better
in 7

better
in 7

The Ultimate Seven-Day Guide to a Better YOU!

Andrew Ordon M.D., F.A.C.S.

Published in Los Angeles, California, by Bird Street Books, Inc.

ISBN: 978-0-9854627-0-3

Disclaimer: This publication is intended to provide helpful and informative material. It is not intended to diagnose, treat, cure, or prevent any health problem or condition, nor is intended to replace the advice of a physician or qualified health-care professional. No action should be taken solely on the contents of this book. Always consult your physician or qualified health-care professional on any matters regarding your health and before adopting any suggestions in this book or drawing inferences from it.

The author, owner, and publisher specifically disclaim all responsibility for any liability, loss, or risk, personal or otherwise, which is incurred as a consequence, directly or indirectly, from the use or application of any contents of this book. Any and all product names referenced within this book are the trademarks of their respective owners. None of these owners have sponsored, authorized, endorsed or approved this book. Always read all information provided by the manufacturers' product labels before using their products. The author, owner, and publisher are not responsible for claims made by manufacturers. The statements made in this book have not been evaluated by the Food and Drug Administration.

This book is dedicated to my two doctors-to-be: my daughter, Shannon, and son, Matthew. I couldn't be prouder that they're following in my footsteps and becoming the next generation of Ordon doctors. And to my beautiful wife, Robyn, who loves and supports me every day.

7

contents

introduction

This very minute, someone is contemplating getting a breast enhancement, a face-lift, or some junk lipo-ed out of her thighs. If that someone is you, stop. Move away from the operating-table mentality, at least for a moment.

You have other alternatives before you go there...even if you think you lost out in the good genes sweepstakes, even if you've got a butt with its own seat in Congress, and even if you haven't felt this ugly since junior high school.

There are so many natural ways to have a prettier face or a better figure, even a better sex life—and I want you to have it all. That's what this book is all about—getting better—in every way that's important to you, in just seven days. I've put *all* of my very best tips, secrets, and insights about how to be more beautiful, youthful, and happy with yourself in this book. They have worked for me. Here's a preview of coming attractions. You'll learn how to:

- Create smooth, flawless skin.
- Lose fat and water weight.
- Get abs that are six-packs, not old sacks.

- Banish age spots, spider veins, and every girl's worst nightmare—cellulite.
- Whiten your teeth.
- Achieve better orgasms.
- Feel more energetic.
- Look and feel seven years younger.
- And much more...all in seven days.

And that's just for starters. Whatever it is about you that you want to change, it's here. I'm going to share some powerful strategies with you that are going to change the way you look and feel. I'm going to tell you exactly what *works* and *what doesn't* when it comes to improving your body and your appearance. I'm going to tell you what things you've probably been doing that you should *avoid* at all costs, because they're appearance *killers*. And I'm going to give you some tips on how to make yourself totally beautiful, sexy, desirable, and youthful.

Now for those of you just making my acquaintance, my name is Dr. Drew Ordon. I'm a plastic and reconstructive surgeon based in Beverly Hills and a host of the popular daytime show *The Doctors*. Mainly, I perform face-lifts, tummy tucks, liposuction, breast augmentation, and other plastic surgery procedures. I'm a board-certified plastic surgeon, as well as a board-certified head and neck surgeon. While most people think plastic surgeons spend the majority of their time performing face-lifts and liposuctions, I like to point out that more than 75 percent of our work is reconstructive—helping people with serious needs resulting from accidents, facial trauma, burns, or congenital defects such as cleft lips and palates. As plastic surgeons, we strive to be good physicians first and good reconstructive surgeons second. And, if we are good physicians and reconstructive surgeons, then we can use our skills to fulfill patients' desires through elective cosmetic surgery, too.

Our specialty really evolved because of injuries and deformities that were the result of battle during World Wars I and II. Many soldiers suffered facial traumas during these wars, and plastic surgery began to develop as a specialty of its own as physicians helped these injured men.

In my occupation, I'm trained in understanding proportions and lines and contours, like an artist, but with the human body as the canvas. I consider myself artistic, and I don't think there's any question plastic surgery is the one specialty that mixes art and medicine. My eye is trained to look at the balance of certain facial features, as well as the proportion of bodies. A great deal of my job satisfaction comes from the feelings that my patients have after I treat them. Sculpting people's faces or bodies and having them say, "I love the way I look," gives me joy.

I fell in love with plastic surgery in med school. I just knew it was the right fit! As medical students, we rotate through each one of the disciplines. We do some pediatrics, we do some psychiatry, we do some OB-GYN. When I did my rotation in plastic surgery, I witnessed the ability of some surgeons to help change patients' appearances for the better. To me, this was the turning point in my education. From then on, I knew what I wanted to do, because I could see how much plastic surgery could improve a person's quality of life.

Okay, I know what you're thinking: Why is a plastic surgeon telling me all this? Yes, I specialize in improving my patients' appearance through surgery, but the idea of going under the knife is not something every woman wants to pursue. Not only are many of these cosmetic procedures temporary, you must repeat them at monthly or yearly intervals. And, depending on what you go for, they aren't cheap. And surgery—cosmetic or otherwise—is very hard on your body. Just because you might be put to sleep during some surgeries doesn't mean it wasn't a traumatic event. Your body doesn't know it is having a medical procedure. It just thinks it has been stabbed a few times. And some cosmetic surgeries can leave you looking like a car crash victim for a couple of weeks.

And often, surgeries like these aren't even appropriate for certain people. To be sure, all patients don't always have the best reasons for undergoing surgery: They may want to look just like a movie star, or at least better than their stuck-up, affected neighbor.

Nowadays, there's so much encouraging news on the skincare, beauty, and fitness front, that I just have to share this information with you. In a rebellion against surgery, the number of elective facial plastic surgery procedures has dropped 35.57% percent over the last 10 years in the United States, according to the American Society of Plastic Surgeons. Instead of scalpels and invasive procedures that can give women a fake appearance, with the wind-tunnel look and chipmunk cheeks, women are reportedly opting for more natural treatments. With them, you can move from "not" to "hot" without having the beauty police ripping you to shreds like hyenas on Animal Planet. This is an exciting time. It's never been easier to look your best. And you don't have to loot your 401k to do it.

Before working on this book, I actually put together a list of concerns that I most commonly get from women like you, who are wondering how to get past certain "bumps" in the road when it comes to their bodies—and every concern is covered in this book, from weight loss to skin to anti-aging to better sex. Whatever you want to improve in seven days, just turn to that section of the book, and I'll show you how.

For example, wouldn't it be great if you could *stop* the patterns you have and the mistakes you've made that have prevented you being the hottest version of yourself?

Wouldn't you *love* to know the secrets behind what really makes a woman more beautiful?

And wouldn't it be great if you could do all this without expensive potions or even plastic surgery?

No matter when you start, you can make a difference in your looks—but don't wait too long. I was once wedged into a small elevator in New York City with two aging actresses, and it was the most frightening experience I ever had in my life: They didn't look a day over 110. Their shriveled-up walnut faces were the result of not taking care of themselves over time. This doesn't have to happen to you!

I've devoted a good deal of my practice to helping women improve their appearance and lives *naturally*. Truth be told, I think I have more knowledge as a plastic surgeon about how a woman should take care of herself than someone behind a cosmetics counter.

I know you have no intention of sliding gracefully into frumpy middle age. Quite simply, there is a lot you can do about it. If you're on board—and I hope you are—I'd like you to get in the right mind-set first. Sooner or later, there isn't a grown woman alive who doesn't scrutinize herself in the mirror and get caught in the negative thinking trap of focusing on what they don't like about their body. I know you're doing it. Don't try to tell me that your negative appraisal of your looks is something you've grown out of; forgotten along with your locker combination, the capital of Montana, and the words to a song that was your favorite in the summer of '87. More than half of all American women really dislike their looks, reported a *Psychology Today* survey.

It's like this: Either you can obsess about things like extra flab or lines on your face (it's *so* not sexy to obsess) or you can zero in on your prettiest features and celebrate the many ways in which you look great (this is *very* sexy). Here's a pep talk: When you look in the mirror, focus first on the features that you actually like (c'mon, there must be a few). Every day, acknowledge you have great skin or pretty eyes before dissing that slightly bigger butt. In other words, view yourself from an admirer's perspective.

Got it? Okay, now on to my seven-day programs: You know that high you get from wearing a hot new type of make-up? Or the thrill of getting a sexy haircut before a date? Those are small-scale examples of what will happen to you after you apply my seven-day programs to your life. Each one that you try will have a huge impact on your psyche, and you'll begin to see yourself in an amazing new light.

And once you start any of the seven-day programs of your choice, every morning when you look in the mirror and see a fresh face and better body looking back at you, you'll feel more beautiful and sexy, inside and out. After just seven days, when the paparazzi are hounding you because you look and feel like a star, just turn toward the camera, wink, and say, "I'll take that as a thank-you."

Now, if that sounds like your kind of "wow" experience, please join me in this adventure toward a better you...in just seven days.

better7

FREE BONUS EXERCISE VIDEOS!

👍 Like US AT FACEBOOK.COM/BETTERIN7 FOR ACCESS

You'll find a complete collection of videos on our Better in 7 Facebook page. They'll show you how to have perfect form on all the simple exercises within the "7 Day Plans" found in the book.

Just visit **facebook.com/betterin7** —"like" our page, and click the "videos" tab at the top of the page!

facebook.com/betterin7

PART 1

better body in 7

There might be a lot of things you do well in your life, but I'm willing to bet that shaping up isn't one of them—which is why you may not be as svelte and toned as you wish. I have a hunch you've tried everything, from celebrity videos to drinking diet shakes and all that. And let me just say these techniques work great, especially if you don't like doing things like, say, breathing or chewing.

A lot of our attempts to get in shape last about four days at best—which is about three-and-a-half days longer than usual. This is why I've abbreviated my "Shapelier in 7" programs into just one week—because you want to get in better shape fast. These programs will show you how to quickly lose weight, trim your abs and thighs, and more.

And I'm not talking only about "camouflaging" figure flaws you might hate. Now, I don't know about you, but my perception of camouflage is clothing the Army puts on to hide from the enemy and blend into the background. If that's the case, bikinis should look like sand and have shells glued on them. I know you don't want to hide anything. You want it to go away. If I'm right, the next few chapters are for you.

CHAPTER 1
thinner in 7

Do you wish you could lose weight fast? How about 10 pounds in seven days? Got a big event coming up? Would you like to drop a dress size by Friday?

Here's my special "Thinner in 7" diet, which is designed to carve off up to 10 pounds in a week, flatten your belly, and even change your shape. Oh, and I should mention that it will leave your face looking years younger, because it's based on natural foods.

But this diet isn't for the lazy. If you want to be every man's (including your husband or boyfriend) object of desire, you need to watch what you eat. No more burgers, shakes, ice cream, doughnuts, sausages, tacos, and fatty fast foods that slap fat on your hips and elsewhere. You'll never see sexy women pig out and eat that kind of junk. It takes determination and desire to look as good as they do.

And here's a plus: You will get results overnight. No woman I've ever talked to wanted to wait weeks on end to start looking more shapely. Women like you want results right away, and this diet delivers—as quickly as the very next day.

At this point, I know you're probably thinking: What the hell does a plastic surgeon know about diet? Fair question—after all, we do body contouring procedures like tummy tucks and liposuction as fast routes to a better body. Do we even care about diet? Yes, we do—big time.

Most plastic surgeons are very in sync with diet and nutrition. We prefer that our patients be within around 5 or 10 pounds of a respectable, healthy weight prior to having any kind of plastic surgery, including liposuction. Performing surgery on very overweight or obese people is risky. I'd rather have you be as fit as possible. Being in shape helps ensure a great outcome, because I can see your best silhouette, and the surgery will go better. I won't take a patient who is very overweight. So, I tell my plastic surgery patients that I will do my part in helping them achieve their desired look, but they must first do their part in practicing healthy eating and exercise habits to ensure they get to a surgery-appropriate weight and then make healthy lifestyle choices to maintain the results of their surgery.

The "Thinner in 7" diet you're about to start is similar to what I use with patients who need to trim off pounds prior to surgery; so, I know it works because I've seen it work.

This diet is based on two principles: calorie manipulation and water manipulation. The calorie manipulation principle has to do with controlling calories. You'll be following a lower-calorie diet; however, it won't feel restrictive, because the foods you'll eat are very filling. Lowering calories forces the body to burn fat for energy, and when you burn fat, your body shape starts to change for the better.

As for water manipulation, the diet is designed to flush your body of toxic water—the stuff that wants to stay around, causing bloat, puffiness, and lots of extra pounds. So, yes, you'll lose water weight. But hey, ladies: Water is weight—ugly, figure-marring weight. I want you to lose it! When you lose water weight, you flatten your belly rapidly, and you'll get into a smaller size effortlessly. Accordingly, the diet emphasizes diuretic foods and natural diuretic supplements that help counteract bloating that occurs when your body tries to retain water. And if your tummy ever sticks out (the result of abdominal bloating), this diet will flatten it rapidly.

Trust me, the day you start this diet, you'll instantly feel less bloated, which is a big factor when it comes to slinking into your sexiest clothes.

The diet offers a balanced and healthy way to eat nutritiously, because you're getting good carbohydrates, beneficial fats, and proteins during the day.

Okay, let me walk you through this diet, day by day. Do exactly as I outline; do not deviate.

Day 1

The first day starts with fruit only because it is a natural way to fuel the body with energy and nutrients. Fruits have terrific fat-burning benefits: they are filling, fat-free, low in calories, and high in fat-fighting fiber, compared to other foods most of us normally eat.

UPON RISING:

Weigh yourself naked. Record your weight on a note card, journal, or other piece of paper. Don't weigh yourself again until the eighth day.

6 TO 7 A.M. (OR WHENEVER YOU NORMALLY GET UP):

Start by microwaving a coffee cup full of water. Squeeze in the juice of one lemon. Sip. This drink helps rehydrate your body after a night's sleep and assists the colon in contracting to expel waste.

WITHIN 30 MINUTES:

For breakfast, have 2 cups of watermelon chunks and 1 cup of green tea.

WITH BREAKFAST:

Take one dose of dandelion root extract (250 milligrams each)*.

Take one dose of bearberry extract (200 milligrams each).**

Take one multivitamin/multimineral tablet.

---

* *Dandelion root helps increase water loss, thanks to active but hard-to-pronounce ingredients called taraxasterols. Taraxasterols accelerate the removal of sodium from the kidneys, and this makes you pee more. Take about 250 milligrams of dandelion root, twice a day.*

** *The leaves of the bearberry plant can help prevent bloat. They contain an active ingredient called arbutin, which also creates more pee. Look for a supplement that provides at least 200 milligrams per dose, and take it twice a day.*

9 A.M.:
Drink 2 cups water; flavor with fresh lemon juice, if desired.

10:30 A.M.:
Drink 8 ounces (1 cup) of coconut water. Coconut water is loaded with the mineral potassium. Potassium flushes out excess water, which means you'll eventually have the flattest tummy in the restroom. Apart from this, many of us doctors believe that coconut water's ability to maintain water balance helps rev up the body's metabolism.

NOON:
Prepare a fruit salad of any of the following:

- ☐ *Option 1*: One large navel orange + one Granny Smith apple + ½ cup of fresh raspberries. Have 1 cup of water, flavored with fresh lemon juice, if desired.

- ☐ *Option 2*: Quarter cantaloupe + 1 cup of fresh pineapple chunks + ½ cup of fresh blueberries. Have 1 cup of water, flavored with fresh lemon juice, if desired.

- ☐ *Option 3*: Half grapefruit + one pear + ½ cup sliced strawberries. Have 1 cup of water, flavored with fresh lemon juice, if desired.

WITH LUNCH:
Take one dose of dandelion root extract (250 milligrams each).

Take one dose of bearberry extract (200 milligrams each).

3 P.M.:
Drink 2 cups water; flavor with fresh lemon juice, if desired.

6 P.M.:
Prepare a fruit salad of any of the following:

- ☐ *Option 1*: One large navel orange + one Granny Smith apple + ½ cup of fresh raspberries. Have 1 cup water, flavored with fresh lemon juice, if desired.

- ☐ *Option 2*: Quarter cantaloupe + 1 cup of fresh pineapple chunks + ½ cup of fresh blueberries. Have 1 cup water, flavored with fresh lemon juice, if desired.

- ☐ *Option 3*: Half grapefruit + one pear + ½ cup sliced strawberries. Have 1 cup water, flavored with fresh lemon juice, if desired.

TIPS TO MAKE DAY 1 SUCCESSFUL

Eat a different combination of fruit at dinner than you did at lunch. This way, you don't get bored eating the same fruits. By boosting your intake of fruits, you're increasing the amount of vitamins and minerals to strengthen your immune system so you won't get sick—everyone hates to get sick—and you'll improve the quality of your skin so that it glows, though not in the dark.

Day 2

6 TO 7 A.M.: (OR WHENEVER YOU NORMALLY GET UP):
Start by microwaving a coffee cup full of water. Squeeze in the juice of one lemon. Sip.

WITHIN 30 MINUTES:
For breakfast, have 2 cups of watermelon chunks or one whole grapefruit or a quarter cantaloupe, and 1 cup of green tea with your meal.

Take one dose of dandelion root extract (250 milligrams each).

Take one dose of bearberry extract (200 milligrams each).

Take one multivitamin/multimineral tablet.

9 A.M.:
Drink 2 cups water; flavor with fresh lemon juice, if desired.

10:30 A.M.:
Drink 8 ounces (1 cup) of coconut water.

NOON:

Prepare a large plate of salad: mixed greens, ½ diced cucumber, ½ cup chopped parsley, one chopped celery stalk, and ½ cup shiitake mushrooms. Spritz the salad with a salad spritzer (such as Wishbone) for flavor. Have 1 cup of water with lunch, flavored with fresh lemon juice, if desired.

Take one dose of dandelion root extract (250 milligrams each).

Take one dose of bearberry extract (200 milligrams each).

3 P.M.:

Drink 2 cups water; flavor with fresh lemon juice, if desired.

6 P.M.:

Prepare a plate of the following steamed vegetables:

- ☐ Ten spears of asparagus
- ☐ ½ cup cooked carrots
- ☐ 1 cup steamed sliced red bell peppers
- ☐ 1 cup water with dinner; flavor with fresh lemon juice, if desired

TIPS TO MAKE DAY 2 SUCCESSFUL

Rather than use salt to flavor your veggies, season them with no-salt herb seasoning. It's fine to spritz them with a few sprays of vegetable cooking spray, if desired. The vegetables you will eat today are for fiber, as well to help eliminate water. Vegetables have a small amount of carbohydrates for energy, but more importantly, they're full of vitamins and minerals.

Day 3

6 TO 7 A.M. (OR WHENEVER YOU NORMALLY GET UP):

Start by microwaving a coffee cup full of water. Squeeze in the juice of one lemon. Sip.

WITHIN 30 MINUTES:

For breakfast, have 2 cups of watermelon chunks or one whole grapefruit or quarter cantaloupe, and 1 cup of green tea.

Take one dose of dandelion root extract (250 milligrams each).

Take one dose of bearberry extract (200 milligrams each).

Take one multivitamin/multimineral tablet.

9 A.M.:
Drink 2 cups of water; flavor with fresh lemon juice, if desired.

10:30 A.M.:
Drink 8 ounces (1 cup) of coconut water.

NOON:
Prepare a large plate of salad: mixed greens, ½ diced cucumber, ½ cup chopped parsley, one chopped celery stalk, and ½ cup shiitake mushrooms. Add to your salad: two hard-boiled eggs, sliced. Spritz the salad with a salad spritzer (such as Wishbone) for flavor. Have one glass of water with lunch, flavored with fresh lemon juice, if desired.

Take one dose of dandelion root extract (250 milligrams each).

Take one dose of bearberry extract (200 milligrams each).

3 P.M.:
Drink 2 cups of water; flavor with fresh lemon juice, if desired.

6 P.M.:
One chicken breast, baked or grilled, plus 1 to 2 cups of steamed vegetables (green beans, yellow wax beans, spinach, turnip greens, dandelion greens, or other greens, summer squash, or zucchini). Have 1 cup of water with dinner, flavored with fresh lemon juice, if desired.

TIPS TO MAKE DAY 3 SUCCESSFUL

Please stick to the vegetables listed. Other common "diet" veggies such as broccoli, cabbage, and cauliflower can cause bloating, so you want to avoid those on this diet. You're almost halfway through—see, that wasn't so hard, was it?

Day 4

6 TO 7 A.M. (OR WHENEVER YOU NORMALLY GET UP):
Start by microwaving a coffee cup full of water. Squeeze in the juice of one lemon. Sip.

WITHIN 30 MINUTES:
For breakfast, have 2 cups of watermelon chunks or one whole grapefruit or quarter cantaloupe, and 1 cup of green tea.

Take one dose of dandelion root extract (250 milligrams each).

Take one dose of bearberry extract (200 milligrams each).

Take one multivitamin/multimineral tablet.

9 A.M.:
Drink 2 cups of water; flavor with fresh lemon juice, if desired.

10:30 A.M.:
Drink 8 ounces (1 cup) of coconut water.

NOON:
Prepare a large plate of salad: mixed greens, ½ diced cucumber, ½ cup chopped parsley, one chopped celery stalk, and ½ cup shiitake mushrooms. Add to your salad: two hard-boiled eggs, sliced. Spritz the salad with a salad spritzer (such as Wishbone) for flavor. Have one glass of water with lunch, flavored with fresh lemon juice, if desired.

Take one dose of dandelion root extract (250 milligrams each).

Take one dose of bearberry extract (200 milligrams each).

3 P.M.:
Drink 2 cups of water; flavor with fresh lemon juice, if desired.

6 P.M.:
One (4- to 5-ounce) grilled sirloin steak or filet mignon, plus 1 to 2 cups of steamed vegetables (asparagus, green beans, yellow wax beans,

spinach, turnip greens, summer squash, or zucchini). Have 1 cup of water with dinner, flavored with fresh lemon juice, if desired.

<u>*TIPS TO MAKE DAY 4 SUCCESSFUL*</u>

If you find yourself feeling hungry between meals, nosh on baby carrots and/or increase your water intake. Thirst often masquerades as hunger.

Day 5

6 TO 7 A.M. (OR WHENEVER YOU NORMALLY GET UP):
Start by microwaving a coffee cup full of water. Squeeze in the juice of one lemon. Sip.

WITHIN 30 MINUTES:
For breakfast, have 2 cups of watermelon chunks or one whole grapefruit or quarter cantaloupe, and 1 cup of green tea.

Take one dose of dandelion root extract (250 milligrams each)

Take one dose of bearberry extract (200 milligrams each)

Take one multivitamin/multimineral tablet

9 A.M.:
Drink 2 cups of water; flavor with fresh lemon juice, if desired.

10:30 A.M.:
Drink 8 ounces (1 cup) of coconut water.

NOON:
Prepare a large plate of salad: mixed greens, ½ diced cucumber, ½ cup chopped parsley, one chopped celery stalk, and ½ cup shiitake mushrooms. Add to your salad: two hard-boiled eggs, sliced. Spritz the salad with a salad spritzer (such as Wishbone) for flavor. Have one glass of water with lunch, flavored with fresh lemon juice, if desired.

Take one dose of dandelion root extract (250 milligrams each)

Take one dose of bearberry extract (200 milligrams each)

3 P.M.:
Drink 2 cups of water; flavor with fresh lemon juice, if desired.

6 P.M.:
One tilapia filet, grilled or baked, plus 1 to 2 cups of steamed vegetables (asparagus, green beans, yellow wax beans, spinach, turnip greens, summer squash, or zucchini). Have 1 cup of water, flavored with fresh lemon juice, if desired.

TIPS TO MAKE DAY 5 SUCCESSFUL

If you're getting bored with steamed veggies, try stir-frying them. Spray a small sauté pan liberally with vegetable cooking spray. Cut the veggies into bite-size pieces and add them to the pan. Stir fry for six to ten minutes, stirring lightly. Add a few tablespoons of water if the vegetables are sticking to the pan.

Day 6

6 TO 7 A.M. (OR WHENEVER YOU NORMALLY GET UP):
Start by microwaving a coffee cup full of water. Squeeze in the juice of one lemon. Sip.

WITHIN 30 MINUTES:
For breakfast, have 2 cups of watermelon chunks or one whole grapefruit or half cantaloupe, and 1 cup of green tea.

Take one dose of dandelion root extract (250 milligrams each).

Take one dose of bearberry extract (200 milligrams each).

Take one multivitamin/multimineral tablet.

9 A.M.:
Drink 2 cups of water; flavor with fresh lemon juice, if desired.

10:30 A.M.:
Drink 8 ounces (1 cup) of coconut water.

NOON:
Prepare a large plate of salad: mixed greens, ½ diced cucumber, ½ cup chopped parsley, one chopped celery stalk, and ½ cup shiitake mushrooms. Add to your salad: two hard-boiled eggs, sliced. Spritz the salad with a salad spritzer (such as Wishbone) for flavor. Have one glass of water with lunch, flavored with fresh lemon juice, if desired.

Take one dose of dandelion root extract (250 milligrams each).

Take one dose of bearberry extract (200 milligrams each).

3 P.M.:
Drink 2 cups of water; flavor with fresh lemon juice, if desired.

6 P.M.:
One chicken breast, baked or grilled, plus 1 to 2 cups of steamed or stir-fried vegetables (asparagus, green beans, yellow wax beans, spinach, turnip greens, summer squash, or zucchini.) Have 1 cup of water with dinner, flavored with lemon juice, if desired.

TIPS TO MAKE DAY 6 SUCCESSFUL

You're almost to the finish line. Pull out one of your smaller sized outfits from the closet (something that was previously too tight, like a pair of jeans or a skirt), and hang it out in the open as visual motivation to get you through the next two days.

Day 7

6 TO 7 A.M. (OR WHENEVER YOU NORMALLY GET UP):
Start by microwaving a coffee cup full of water. Squeeze in the juice of one lemon. Sip.

WITHIN 30 MINUTES:

For breakfast, have 2 cups of watermelon chunks or one whole grape-fruit or quarter cantaloupe, and 1 cup of green tea.

Take one dose of dandelion root extract (250 milligrams each).

Take one dose of bearberry extract (200 milligrams each).

Take one multivitamin/multimineral tablet.

9 A.M.:

Drink 2 cups of water; flavor with fresh lemon juice, if desired.

10:30 A.M.:

Drink 8 ounces (1 cup) of coconut water.

NOON:

Prepare a large plate of salad: mixed greens, ½ diced cucumber, ½ cup chopped parsley, one chopped celery stalk, and ½ cup shii-take mushrooms. Add to your salad: two hard-boiled eggs, sliced. Spritz the salad with a salad spritzer (such as Wishbone) for flavor. Have one glass of water with lunch, flavored with fresh lemon juice, if desired.

Take one dose of dandelion root extract (250 milligrams each).

Take one dose of bearberry extract (200 milligrams each).

3 P.M.:

Drink 2 cups of water; flavor with fresh lemon juice, if desired.

6 P.M.:

Prepare a plate of the following steamed or stir-fried vegetables:

- 10 spears of asparagus
- ½ cup cooked carrots
- 1 cup steamed, sliced red bell peppers

Congratulations, this is your last day! You may be tempted to throw in the towel, but don't! Treat yourself to a manicure, pedicure, facial, or body treatment today. Feel good about yourself, because tomorrow you're going to slip effortlessly into that skimpier outfit.

Day 8 and Beyond

Please weigh yourself naked first thing in the morning. Try on that outfit. _Voila!_—step back from the mirror and congratulate yourself on how fabulous you look.

If you want to continue the "Thinner in 7" diet for another seven days, you have my blessing. But beyond that, stick to a prudent diet that's high in veggies, moderate in protein and fat, and low in carbs. Feel free to use the "Thinner in 7" diet when you need to slim down quickly, but no more than twice a month. With continued sensible eating and exercise, you should have no problem getting your weight off and keeping that weight off.

CHAPTER 3

CHAPTER 2
flatter tummy in 7

Muffin top. Now to those of you lucky few who don't know what this, I'll tell you. It used to be that the phrase "muffin top" referred to the top part of a baked muffin. Harmless enough. But now, it means the hideous bulge of flab around your tummy that overlaps your waistband, for the whole world to see, when you wear low-rise jeans.

The muffin top is the area I get asked about quite frequently. If a woman wants cosmetic surgery to treat it, I typically use liposuction and/or a tummy tuck for body contouring.

But while cosmetic surgery may be the answer to jiggling tummies, there's no doubt it can be beyond most budgets. If your purse isn't as big as your bulge, there are ways to achieve results, without massive cost. Let's talk about this.

Now if you're the sort of person who can't pass up something that promises big results with minimal effort, there are two things you can do right away for an "instant tummy tuck."

First, wear Spanx or some other brand of super-firming underwear. My wife wears this stuff all the time, and she tells me no woman is complete without it. Like a wetsuit, it takes a few minutes to wiggle in, and it might feel like you're reeling in a large marlin, but once it's in place, there's no muffin top. Second, stand or sit up straight, with your shoulders back and belly tucked in. Good posture will slim your midsection instantly.

I have some other strategies that will take the bulge right off you, fast, and they make up part of my seven-day tummy-trimming program. Here's an overview of what you'll need.

Workout Strategies

Purchase a Pilates DVD, and do the routine several times a week. Pilates tones your entire body but with concentration on your core (middle section and abs) and improves your flexibility.

Then, perform proper crunches at least three times a week for your abs. Shoot for about 50 each time. Avoid sit-ups because they don't do much to firm your belly muscles. Sit-ups work your hip muscles more than anything else.

Along with crunches, do an exercise called the *plank* to strengthen your midsection. Lie facedown on the floor, with your hands on the floor or mat about shoulder-width apart. Your toes should be touching the floor, too. Push up so that you're holding yourself in an almost-straight line to the floor. Hold for 15 to 20 seconds two or three times; repeat three times a week.

Do some cardio activity through the week because certain types of cardio exercise could actually target the waistline. It's true! Researchers at the Washington University School of Medicine in St. Louis, Missouri, put a group of men and women, aged 60 to 70 on a 9- to 12-month exercise program that consisted of walking or jogging. On average, the subjects exercised 45 minutes several times a week. By the end of the study, both the men and the women had lost weight. But get this: Most of their weight was shed from the abdominal area. This tells me that a simple exercise routine like walking or jogging can melt off abdominal fat.

Based on this information, the best flab-busting aerobics for your midsection include walking, jogging or running, or treadmill exercise. Try to perform aerobic exercises five times a week for best results.

Nutritional Strategies

Add fiber to your diet, and cut down your intake of the bad carbs. Limit your intake of foods like white bread, pastas, potatoes, and white rice. When you cut back on the carbs in your diet, you temporarily train your body to access stored fat and burn it off, while also urinating out excess stored fluids.

Also, most starches, including potatoes, corn, pasta, and wheat, produce gas because they are broken down in the large intestine. Rice is the only starch that doesn't cause gas, so have a ½-cup serving of brown rice (which has more fiber) if you want carbs with dinner.

To get more fiber, increase your intake of fresh fruits, but not just any fruits. Eat fruits that are kinder on your belly. Berries, grapes, and citrus contain a near-equal ratio of the sugars fructose and glucose, making them easier to digest than fruits with more fructose, such as honeydew, apples, and pears.

Forget drinking cow's milk, even skim milk. Have coconut milk, rice milk, or almond milk instead. Dairy products often cause abdominal bloating and gas. If you must have any type of dairy product, go with yogurt. It's great for digestion. What's more, I have reams of research in my office showing that yogurt, when used with a low-calorie diet, helps reduce fat around the waistline.

Here's something else important: The type of fat you're eating really matters, according to recent studies. A diet high in monounsaturated fat specifically appears to decrease abdominal fat. Trade out saturated fats like butter for these good fats. They're found in foods like nuts, olives, avocados, and olive oil and should be eaten every day. They encourage your body to burn fat around your middle, giving you a toned, flat tummy.

Take a supplemental fat called *conjugated linoleic acid* (CLA). CLA is a type of naturally occurring fat found in dairy products and meat. A study published in the *International Journal of Obesity* shows that CLA can actually help you burn off belly fat, even during holiday-season feeding frenzies. For the study, researchers at the University of Guelph and the University of Wisconsin – Madison recruited 40 overweight but otherwise healthy volunteers. Half of them were given a daily supplement of 3.2 grams of CLA for a six-month period that overlapped with the year-end holiday season. The others got placebo (look-alike) pills. Over the course of the study, the CLA group lost an average of 2.2 pounds of fat, especially around the belly. By contrast, those in the placebo group gained 1.5 pounds during the holiday. CLA is by no means a "miracle" pill. But it seems to work, if used in combination with sensible eating and regular exercise.

Go salt-free. Eating too much salt makes you retain more fluid, contributing to a puffy appearance and extra water weight. So, avoid salt, over-processed foods, and salt-based seasonings. As an alternative, add zest to your dinner recipes with fresh herbs and salt-free seasoning blends such as the Original and Italian Medley Mrs. Dash.

Hold the hot. If you love the four-alarm stuff, lay off the hot sauce, jalapenos, and garlic for a few days while de-bloating. Spicy foods stimulate the release of stomach acid, causing irritation. Flavor foods with fresh or dried herbs such as dill, basil, mint, sage, tarragon, and rosemary. Try curry powder or lemon or lime juice with fish or chicken.

Watch out for gluten. If you're sensitive to gluten, a protein in wheat-based carbs, it can weaken your abdominal wall and make it slack, resulting in a tummy that sticks out. Foods containing gluten include bread and pasta (unless gluten-free), most breakfast cereals, many baked goods, and alcohol made from grains, such as beer, whiskey, bourbon, and liqueurs.

Drink plenty of water. You should be drinking six to eight glasses a day, at least. Not only will it help fill you up so you eat less, but it also aids in digestion.

Steer clear of alcohol for the next seven days to maximize your body's belly-flattening capabilities. Alcohol causes dehydration and may slow your body's ability to eliminate that excess waste, so if you had a little too much to drink this weekend, start chugging the H$_2$O.

Take a bath. Lots of my model clients take an Epsom salts bath just before a bathing suit or lingerie photo shoot. Epsom salts are an ancient remedy for drawing out toxins. Just add one or 2 cups of Epsom salts (available at most pharmacies) to a hot bath.

Now here's how to put these strategies into my seven-day plan.

Day 1

Starting today, write down all the foods you eat. Be 100 percent honest! Research shows that keeping track of what you eat makes you more likely to make nutritious choices and stay on course with your diet. If you find yourself wanting or eating foods that adversely affect your tummy, get rid of them or avoid them.

Breakfast: Eat a high-fiber breakfast (1 cup of All Bran or Fiber One, for example), with 1 cup of coconut milk.

Sip green tea throughout the day. Packed with disease-fighting antioxidants, green tea has mild diuretic properties, so it helps the body get rid of excess water and eases gas. Studies have also shown it may help reduce sugar cravings.

Lunch: Have a lunch of a good carb (like brown rice) with protein and some steamed veggies. Take a daily probiotic capsule with lunch to counteract bloating.

Dinner: Enjoy a raw salad of lettuce, avocado, carrots, cucumbers, and grapes. Dress it with a little olive oil. This has a very cleansing effect.

Supplement with 3 grams of CLA, taken with a meal (this improves absorption).

Walk or jog for 30 to 45 minutes today to boost your metabolism in order to burn belly fat.

Perform 50 crunches today, followed by three sets of planks (hold each plank for 15 to 20 seconds). Be sure to pull your belly button in toward your spine as you perform each crunch and plank.

Stop eating within three hours of bedtime. Your belly will be flatter in the morning.

ADDITIONAL ACTIONS

Take fish oil supplements regularly. They turn on fat-burning hormones and turn off fat-storing hormones. Begin by taking one 1,000-milligram capsule a day with meals and build up to three.

 Day 2

Breakfast: Eat a high-fiber breakfast (1 cup of All Bran or Fiber One, for example), with 1 cup of coconut milk.

Sip green tea throughout the day.

Lunch: Have a lunch of a good carb (like brown rice) with protein and some steamed veggies. Take a daily probiotic capsule with lunch.

Dinner: Enjoy a raw salad of lettuce, avocado, carrots, cucumbers, and grapes. Dress it with a little olive oil.

Supplement with 3 grams of CLA, taken with a meal.

Do your Pilates DVD today or attend a Pilates class.

Stop eating within three hours of bedtime.

ADDITIONAL ACTIONS

Avoid carbonated or fizzy drinks; they cause abdominal bloating and gas. Stop chewing gum too. A big cause of gas and bloating is swallowed air, which you gulp when you chew gum. And speaking of chewing, chew each bite of food at least 15 times. It sounds like a pain, but unchewed food is a big cause of tummy bloat.

 Day 3

Breakfast: Eat a high-fiber breakfast (1 cup of All Bran or Fiber One, for example), with 1 cup of coconut milk.

Sip green tea throughout the day.

Lunch: Have a lunch of a good carb (like brown rice) with protein and some steamed veggies. Take a daily probiotic capsule with lunch.

Dinner: Enjoy a raw salad of lettuce, avocado, carrots, cucumbers, and grapes. Dress it with a little olive oil.

Supplement with 3 grams of CLA, taken with a meal.

Walk or jog for 30 minutes today to boost your metabolism in order to burn belly fat.

Perform 50 crunches today, followed by three sets of planks (hold each plank for 15 to 20 seconds).

Have a massage today, because it releases toxins and calming, feel-good hormones into the body.

Stop eating within three hours of bedtime.

ADDITIONAL ACTIONS

Pack in plenty of potassium, a natural diuretic. It helps speed your digestive system and keeps your stomach from looking like a blowfish. Good sources include chicken and citrus fruits, such as oranges and grapefruit. Portobello mushrooms are loaded with potassium too.

Day 4

Breakfast: Eat a high-fiber breakfast (1 cup of All Bran or Fiber One, for example), with 1 cup of coconut milk.

Sip green tea throughout the day.

Lunch: Have a lunch of a good carb (like brown rice) with protein and some steamed veggies. Take a daily probiotic capsule with lunch.

Dinner: Enjoy a raw salad of lettuce, avocado, carrots, cucumbers, and grapes. Dress it with a little olive oil.

Supplement with 3 grams of CLA, taken with a meal.

Do your Pilates DVD today or attend a Pilates class.

Stop eating within three hours of bedtime.

Get screened for cholesterol, triglycerides, and glucose. Studies have found that people with excess abdominal (or visceral) fat are more than three times as likely to develop heart disease, even after taking into account differences in age, smoking, weight, and other risks for heart disease.

Day 5

Breakfast: Eat a high-fiber breakfast (1 cup of All Bran or Fiber One, for example), with 1 cup of coconut milk.

Sip green tea throughout the day.

Lunch: Have a lunch of a good carb (like brown rice) with protein and some steamed veggies. Take a daily probiotic capsule with lunch.

Dinner: Enjoy a raw salad of lettuce, avocado, carrots, cucumbers, and grapes. Dress it with a little olive oil.

Supplement with 3 grams of CLA, taken with a meal.

Walk or jog for 30 minutes today to boost your metabolism in order to burn belly fat.

If the weekend is coming up, go for a body wrap at a salon. Just one treatment can help you slip back into a pair of slightly too tight jeans. It will help you shed excess fluid and toxins you may be carrying.

Stop eating within three hours of bedtime.

Add the "bicycle" to your abdominal exercise repertoire: Lie on your back on the floor or on an exercise mat. Press your lower back to the mat. Place your hands beside your head, elbows out. Bring your knees up to about a 45-degree angle and slowly go through a bicycle pedal motion. Lift your upper body slightly and twist so that you touch your left elbow to your right knee. Then do the same, touching your right elbow to your left knee, as you alternate straightening your legs, while constantly pulling your belly button in toward your spine. Research shows that this ab exercise is one of the most effective for toning your abs.

Day 6

Breakfast: Eat a high-fiber breakfast (1 cup of All Bran or Fiber One, for example), with 1 cup of coconut milk.

Sip green tea throughout the day.

Lunch: Have a lunch of a good carb (like brown rice) with protein and some steamed veggies. Take a daily probiotic capsule with lunch.

Dinner: Enjoy a raw salad of lettuce, avocado, carrots, cucumbers, and grapes. Dress it with a little olive oil.

Supplement with 3 grams of CLA, taken with a meal.

Do your Pilates DVD today or attend a Pilates class.

Stop eating within three hours of bedtime.

ADDITIONAL ACTIONS

While you're trimming your tummy, start wearing slenderizing jeans that are specially constructed with corset-like stretch panels in front.

Day 7

Breakfast: Eat a high-fiber breakfast (1 cup of All Bran or Fiber One, for example), with 1 cup of coconut milk.

Sip green tea throughout the day.

Lunch: Have a lunch of a good carb (like brown rice) with protein and some steamed veggies. Take a daily probiotic capsule with lunch.

Walk or jog for 30 minutes today to boost your metabolism in order to burn belly fat.

Dinner: For dinner have a raw salad of lettuce, avocado, carrots, cucumbers, and grapes. Dress it with a little olive oil.

Supplement with 3 grams of CLA, taken with a meal.

Perform 50 crunches today, followed by three sets of planks (hold each plank for 15 to 20 seconds).

Stop eating within three hours of bedtime.

Challenge yourself and keep going. To get more results, boost the intensity of your workout as soon as the exercises start feeling easier by adding a few more reps or sets.

Every few days, look at your tummy in the mirror, particularly in the morning. Notice how much flatter it is becoming. A flat stomach comes with a total lifestyle change—not just from doing crunches or even getting plastic surgery. You have to work at it daily and remain consistent with your diet and exercise.

bigger boobs in 7

If you've been unhappy with what nature has given you—ahem, breasts so small that you can't even wear push-up bras because there's nothing to push up— I'll admit that the quickest remedy is breast augmentation surgery, or the "boob job," as it is commonly known.

Getting breast implants requires surgery, and all surgery carries risks, including pain, scarring, and infection. Other, less-common side effects of this procedure include hardening of the breasts due to contraction of scar tissue and rupturing of the implant. Twenty-five percent of women who have undergone breast augmentation may need to have a secondary breast revision. Then there's the cost factor: A good boob job goes for around $7,500.

Should you not want to surrender yourself to a surgeon's knife, there is a natural option—though not as dramatic as having a boob job. But before I talk about it, let me be up front about something: None of the widely advertised bust-enhancing products you see on the Internet and elsewhere will make your boobs bigger.

These products contain a variety of ingredients, including saw palmetto, dong quai, chaste-tree berry, wild yam, fennel, black cohosh, and fenugreek. Several of these herbs are hormonally active and can mess up your body's own hormone balance. Some bust-enhancing dietary supplements contain a fungus that produces a potent estrogen that has been associated with breast enlargement in humans and other species. I don't know about you, but the only fungus I'll ingest is a mushroom (preferably sautéed in a little olive oil and white wine). Basically, I discourage the use of these products because no clinical trials have been conducted on them, and they may be unsafe for long-term use.

The best way to naturally enhance your bust is something pretty simple: strength-training exercises. There are exercises you can do to make sure that your breasts are naturally beautiful, and even a little bigger. They tone the muscle underneath the breast tissue so your chest may appear to be bigger.

Breast tissue is mostly fat; it's not muscle, so you can't firm your breasts through exercise. But with the right strength exercises, you can develop the underlying muscles, the pectorals. Developing these muscles helps lift your breasts, giving the illusion of younger, perkier breasts.

These are also the muscles that breast implants are inserted under or over. So, it makes sense that working these muscles would help make your breasts look bigger, even if you already have implants.

The exercises are basically resistance exercises designed to build the muscles under the breasts. According to the American Council on Exercise, a person can gain up to 1 pound of muscle in seven days. If you concentrate on your chest (pectoral) muscles, some of that gain will be in your chest region.

You also have to do exercises that will strengthen your back and shoulder muscles. This type of workout helps you stand straighter, with your shoulders pulled back, giving the illusion of perky breasts. The benefit is the improvement these exercises will make in your posture.

My seven-day breast-enhancing routine will strengthen and tone the pectoral muscles that are attached to the suspensory ligaments of the breast, aka Cooper's Ligaments. This will give your breasts perfect lift and provide a great boob boost by thickening the pad of muscle on which your breasts sit.

➡ OTHER NATURAL WAYS TO ENHANCE YOUR BREASTS

Here are other ways to enhance your breasts naturally:

- **Manage your weight.** If you look slimmer, your breasts will look proportionally bigger.

- **Watch your posture.** Good posture will also help make the most of your breasts. So, stand and sit straight; if you are slumped or hunched, your breasts will appear much diminished.

- **Find the perfect bra.** A well-fitting bra is your breast's best friend; it will help stop your breasts from sagging, and a well-chosen one will give you great shape.

- **Use Bring It Up sticky pads.** They add volume and lift to your bust by lifting the breast tissue and repositioning the nipple for a fuller, more youthful appearance.

- **Stay away from black or dark-colored tops; they are less likely to show shape.** Plunging necklines are an obvious choice or a form-fitting button-down collared shirt.

Chest Exercises

DUMBBELL BENCH PRESS

This exercise will solve two worrisome figure problems: a "flat" chest and sagging breasts. It does this by building up your pectoral muscles, the muscular foundation upon which your breasts lie. On flat-chested figures, the result is a muscular cleavage that looks alluring. For a larger-breasted woman whose breasts sag, the bench press firms the muscles underneath the bosom to create a lifted appearance.

Lie back on a flat exercise bench and hold a dumbbell in each hand. Your palms should face in the direction of your feet. Position the dumbbells at the sides of your chest. From this point, press the dumbbells up to a position just above your chest. Lock your elbows out at the top. Slowly lower the dumbbells to the starting position, and repeat the exercise for the suggested number of repetitions.

CHEST CIRCLES

This is an excellent firming exercise for the chest, especially the outer segments. Chest circles also develop flexibility in the upper body.

To begin, take a dumbbell in each hand, and lie back on a flat bench. With the palms of your hands facing inward, hold the dumbbells next to the side of each thigh. The top of each dumbbell should be facing upward. In a circular motion, bring the dumbbells out and around past your midsection and chest until they meet together behind your head. During this movement, you should turn your hands so that your palms face upward. Return to the starting position, following the same circular path used in the beginning phase of the exercise. Repeat the movement using the suggested number of repetitions.

CHAIR PUSH-UPS

Lie on the floor face down with your body straight. Elevate your legs by placing the front of your ankles on a chair seat. Position your arms at each side of your chest. Keeping your body straight, press up until your arms are fully extended and your elbows locked. Lower your body slowly to the starting position. Perform as many repetitions as you can. Concentrate on using the strength of your chest muscles throughout the exercise.

FLOOR DUMBBELL FLY

Lie on your back on the floor, and hold a dumbbell in each hand. Begin with your arms stretched out to your sides at shoulder level. Bend your elbows slightly, and bring the dumbbells toward each other in a semicircular movement until they touch over your chest. Slowly return to the starting position. Repeat the exercise as many times as you can.

Back and Shoulder Exercises

DUMBBELL PULLOVER

Position your body crosswise to an exercise bench with your upper back resting on the bench and your knees bent. Hold a dumbbell over your body, with your arms extended. Bend your elbows slightly, and slowly bring the dumbbell back over your head. Try to get a good stretch in your upper back muscles. Return the dumbbell to the starting position, and repeat the exercise for the suggested number of repetitions.

BENT-OVER DUMBBELL ROW

Perform this exercise in front of a mirror to make sure you're in positioned correctly. Begin with two dumbbells on the floor. Bend over so that your back is parallel to the floor but with a slight arch. Your knees should be bent slightly. Grasp the dumbbells in each hand with an overhand grip. Lift and pull the dumbbells into the sides of your chest. In this position, squeeze the muscles of your upper back. Lower the dumbbells slowly to the starting position, and continue for the suggested number of repetitions.

UPRIGHT ROW

Grasp a barbell with your hands about shoulder-width apart. Keeping the bar close to your body, lift it to a position just above your shoulders. Lower slowly to the starting position, and repeat the exercise for the suggested number of repetitions.

DUMBBELL SHOULDER PRESS

This exercise is truly one of the best for widening the shoulder line. The shoulder is a three-headed muscle, and this shoulder press works all three heads, plus the trapezius muscle of the upper back.

Grasp a dumbbell in each hand and hold them at shoulder level, at your sides. Slowly press them upward, locking your elbows at the top. Return to the starting position, and continue the exercise for the suggested number of repetitions.

SIDE LATERAL RAISES

You can perform this exercise in a seated or standing position. To begin the exercise, hold a dumbbell in each hand held at your sides. Keeping your elbows slightly bent, raise the dumbbells up at your sides to a shoulder-level position. Lower, and repeat for the suggested number of repetitions.

 # Day 1

CHEST ROUTINE

EXERCISES	SETS	REPS
Dumbbell Bench Press	2 or 3	12 to 15
Chest Circles	2 or 3	12 to 15
Chair Push-Ups	2 or 3	12 to 15
Floor Dumbbell Fly	2 or 3	12 to 15

 # Day 2

BACK AND SHOULDER ROUTINE

EXERCISES	SETS	REPS
Dumbbell Pullover	2 or 3	12 to 15
Bent-Over Dumbbell Row	2 or 3	12 to 15
Upright Row	2 or 3	12 to 15
Dumbbell Shoulder Press	2 or 3	12 to 15
Side Lateral Raises	2 or 3	12 to 15

 # Day 3

CHEST ROUTINE

EXERCISES	SETS	REPS
Dumbbell Bench Press	2 or 3	12 to 15
Chest Circles	2 or 3	12 to 15
Chair Push-Ups	2 or 3	12 to 15
Floor Dumbbell Fly	2 or 3	12 to 15

Day 4

BACK AND SHOULDER ROUTINE

EXERCISES	SETS	REPS
Dumbbell Pullover	2 or 3	12 to 15
Bent-Over Dumbbell Row	2 or 3	12 to 15
Upright Row	2 or 3	12 to 15
Dumbbell Shoulder Press	2 or 3	12 to 15
Side Lateral Raises	2 or 3	12 to 15

 # Day 5

CHEST ROUTINE

EXERCISES	SETS	REPS
Dumbbell Bench Press	2 or 3	12 to 15
Chest Circles	2 or 3	12 to 15
Chair Push-Ups	2 or 3	12 to 15
Floor Dumbbell Fly	2 or 3	12 to 15

 # Day 6

BACK AND SHOULDER ROUTINE

EXERCISES	SETS	REPS
Dumbbell Pullover	2 or 3	12 to 15
Bent-Over Dumbbell Row	2 or 3	12 to 15
Upright Row	2 or 3	12 to 15
Dumbbell Shoulder Press	2 or 3	12 to 15
Side Lateral Raises	2 or 3	12 to 15

▦ Day 7

CHEST ROUTINE

Exercises	Sets	Reps
Dumbbell Bench Press	2 or 3	12 to 15
Chest Circles	2 or 3	12 to 15
Chair Push-Ups	2 or 3	12 to 15
Floor Dumbbell Fly	2 or 3	12 to 15

Tips

☐ The previous exercises can be done at home or the gym. Proper form is important to avoid injury and for maximum results.

☐ Increase weight, sets, or reps when exercise gets easy.

☐ It's not unusual to feel a bit inadequate when your body doesn't look like those of the sexy babes in men's magazines. Do these exercises consistently, and you'll start feeling more feminine and sexier.

thinner thighs in 7

You're standing in your closet, searching for a decent outfit that fits over your thighs. So far, you've tried on a pair of black pants that you couldn't zip up, a long sweater that made you look like tent, and a beige skirt that felt promising until you tried to sit down and discovered your thighs draping over the sides and down your chair. It is just one of those days. If you're nodding your head in agreement, you're not alone.

I once randomly polled my female patients about their least favorite body part, and a majority pointed to their thighs. Slim, sexy thighs are the dream of many women. Sure, liposuction is an option if you have the resources, but there are inherent risks involved. You might lose some nerve cells with the fat. There's the possibility of a slight, permanent swelling in the areas where the surgeon sucks out pockets of yuck from your thighs, not to mention that you have to wear compression shorts with an elimination hole for the first week after surgery. And you won't really obtain the body of a fit 20-year-old. So much for quick fixes. The alternative is to use my seven-day plan outlined for you here.

Culling from the scientific literature, I designed a two-pronged slimming plan to start trimming inches from your thighs. Simply follow my diet suggestions, and do my recommended workouts, and you'll be ready to slip into smaller jeans pretty damn soon. Here's an overview.

My "Thinner Thighs" Diet: How It Works

In women, a high-fiber diet has been shown to reduce estrogen in the body. Estrogen is a hormone that, among other functions, directs fat to the thighs and hips. Scientists are not sure, but they think that by reducing estrogen naturally, with fiber, less fat gets deposited on the lower body. The key here is to increase the fiber in your diet.

The amount of fiber required to help reduce thigh circumference is at least 26 grams a day. It is generally recommended that adults get 25 to 35 grams of fiber a day anyway. Among the best choices are foods such as beans, peas, and lentils; rice, oat, barley, corn, and wheat bran; pears, apples, oranges, and berries; carrots, potatoes, and squash; corn; seeds; nuts; whole-grain breads, cereals, and pasta; and green beans, broccoli, spinach, and tomatoes.

Here's a study that really impressed me: researchers at the University of Melbourne, Australia, found that people who followed a fiber-rich, high-carbohydrate, low-fat (HCLF) diet were able to lose most of their fat from the lower body (legs and glutes). What this means to those of you who have a difficult time losing lower-body fat: Follow a high-fiber, low-fat diet.

Another important point is to steer clear of fatty foods and foods high in sugar, especially if you are a woman. High-fat foods pack more calories and can more easily be stored as fat on the lower body.

The diet you'll follow here is based on this research. You'll go on a low-calorie, satisfying, high-fiber diet, proportioned for losing thigh fat. The bottom line for your bottom line is that what you put in your stomach will ultimately help you trim your thighs.

A few tips before moving on:

☐ Drink two glasses of good water (filtered, or spring water) after you first get up, before you do anything else. Drink at least eight more glasses of water throughout the day.

☐ Eliminate all sugar or sugar products, except for whole fruit. Truvia is allowed. Truvia is made from the stevia plant and is considered an herb. It tastes sweet but contains no sugar and no calories. Avoid all artificial sweeteners, including aspartame. No corn syrup, honey, or maple syrup. No alcohol of any kind.

☐ At the end of seven days, you will be thinner and less bloated and will feel better in general. You will have fewer cravings. If you want to continue to lose weight and inches, you can stay on this regimen for as long as you like.

MY THIGH-SLIMMING WORKOUT

The best way to work off weight and flab from your thighs is to combine cardio exercise with resistance training. Cardio exercise torches the fat, while resistance training improves muscle tone and strength and firms up your thighs, and the flab goes away. Elliptical training, brisk walking, running, and bicycling are all effective cardio workouts that burn calories and slim down your thighs at the same time.

My regimen includes both types of exercise. Follow it, and you'll be on your way to slimmer, sleeker thighs.

Here are the resistance exercises you'll do.

Chair Squat

Stand in front of a chair with your back toward the chair. Then slowly sit down in the chair, just barely touching the seat. Return to the starting position. Do 3 sets of 15 repetitions.

Semi Squat

Stand sideways at your kitchen counter or next to a chair with your feet spread about shoulder-width apart. Hold on to the counter or chair with your hand, and then slowly squat down until your knees are parallel to the floor. Keep your back straight and your shoulders and knees in line above your toes. Then come back up. Do 3 sets of 15 repetitions.

Leg Lifts

Lie on your side with your legs extended straight out. Cradle your head in your hand with your arm bent. Slowly raise your top leg so it is perpendicular to the floor. Repeat 15 times for each leg.

Plie Squats

Place your feet wider than shoulder-width apart and point your toes outward. Square your shoulders, and keep your chest up. Bend your knees, and lower your hips down toward the floor. Once your thighs are parallel to the floor, push up to the starting position. Repeat for 3 sets of 15 reps.

Reverse Sculpting Lunge

Place your feet hip-width apart and put your hands on your hips. Step back with your right foot about a stride's length. Bend your knees until your right thigh is perpendicular to the floor and your left thigh is parallel to it. Slowly return to starting position. Then repeat with your other leg. Alternate left and right lunges. One on each leg makes a complete rep.

WORTH A TRY: GO FRENCH

There are lots of reasons French women don't get fat, and one is that they are very body- and beauty conscious. Moms start their daughters on a full skincare regimen at the age of 10 or 11, so good grooming is just something that's ingrained in their culture.

One French product to consider for thigh slimming is Elancyl Cellu Reverse Slimming Serum. In 2004, the National Institute for Consumer Protection in France did some research on various beauty products and confirmed that this brand may actually work, producing visibly smoother skin and measurably thinner thighs in just 14 days. It contains an active slimming ingredient, xanthoxyline, that supposedly urges the body to burn existing fat. I do know that France has some of the most advanced beauty labs in the world, and although I can't vouch for the product, I'd say that it's worth a try.

Now for my complete seven-day program.

Day 1

Measure your thighs at their widest girth before you start. By Day 7, you should notice that your thighs will not only shrink but will become smoother.

Breakfast: Fruit salad. Cut up 1 apple and 1 pear. Add a dollop of low-fat Greek yogurt.

Lunch: 1½ cups of vegetarian chili.

Dinner: 3 to 4 ounces of salmon; ½ cup of brown rice; 1 large tossed salad with 2 tablespoons of low-fat salad dressing.

Exercise: Walk as briskly as possible for 30 to 45 minutes. Don't walk on incline roads or hills, because this can make leg muscles grow, and they will look thicker.

At night: Apply Elancyl Cellu Reverse Slimming Serum on your thighs.

Day 2

Breakfast: 1 cup of high-fiber bran cereal (such as All Bran or Fiber One), with 1 cup of coconut milk. Add a handful of fresh berries.

Lunch: Two low-carb tortillas, each filled with ½ cup black beans or ½ cup pinto beans and salsa. 1 cup baby carrots.

Dinner: 3 to 4 ounces of beef tenderloin; 2 cups of steamed broccoli or cauliflower.

Exercise: Perform my thigh-slimming workout.

Day 3

Breakfast: ¾ cup of oatmeal, microwaved with water and 1 mashed banana.

Lunch: Mixed green salad topped with ¾ cup garbanzo beans and 2 tablespoons low-fat salad dressing.

Dinner: Grilled chicken breast, 1 medium baked sweet potato, and 1 cup steamed green beans.

Exercise: Walk as briskly as possible for 30 to 45 minutes. Don't walk on incline roads or hills, because this can make leg muscles grow, and they will look thicker.

At night: Apply Elancyl Cellu Reverse Slimming Serum on your thighs.

📅 Day 4

Breakfast: Two slices of high-fiber whole-grain bread with 2 slices of turkey bacon; 1 pear.

Lunch: Pinto bean chili: ½ cup cooked pinto beans, ½ cup lean ground turkey or beef, 1 cup stewed chopped tomatoes, 2 tablespoons fresh onions.

Dinner: Steamed or boiled shrimp, 2 tablespoons cocktail sauce, ½ cup corn (cooked), tossed salad of 2 cups leaf lettuce, 1 green pepper (chopped), ½ cup raw shredded carrot, ¼ cup onion (chopped), and 2 tablespoons reduced-fat French dressing.

Exercise: Perform my thigh-slimming workout.

📅 Day 5

Breakfast: ½ cup dried prunes and 1 slice of high-fiber wheat bread, plain.

Lunch: Hummus: ½ cup chick peas (pureed and mixed with 1 teaspoon olive oil) and served on cucumber slices; 1 tomato, sliced.

Dinner: Turkey breast, baked or grilled; 1 cup green beans, boiled or steamed.

Exercise: Walk as briskly as possible for 30 to 45 minutes. Don't walk on incline roads or hills, because this can make leg muscles grow, and they will look thicker.

At night: Apply Elancyl Cellu Reverse Slimming Serum on your thighs.

📅 Day 6

Breakfast: ½ cup oat bran cereal, cooked; 1 pear.

Lunch: Extra lean hamburger patty; ½ cup commercial three-bean salad, drained.

Dinner: Two lamb chops, baked or grilled; broccoli, steamed or boiled; tossed salad of 2 cups leaf lettuce, 1 green pepper (chopped), ½ cup raw shredded carrot, ¼ cup onion (chopped), and 2 tablespoons reduced-fat French dressing.

Exercise: Perform my thigh-slimming workout.

At night: Apply Elancyl Cellu Reverse Slimming Serum on your thighs.

Day 7

Breakfast: 1 cup of high-fiber bran cereal (such as All Bran or Fiber One), with 1 cup of coconut milk. Add a handful of fresh berries.

Lunch: One bowl commercial low-fat vegetable soup; 1 slice high-fiber whole-wheat bread.

Dinner: Tilapia, baked; Caesar salad: 1 cup chopped Romaine lettuce, 6 tablespoons shredded raw carrot, ½ cup chopped cucumber, and 2 tablespoons fat-free Caesar salad dressing

Exercise: Walk as briskly as possible for 30 to 45 minutes. Don't walk on incline roads or hills, because this can make leg muscles grow, and they will look thicker.

At night: Apply Elancyl Cellu Reverse Slimming Serum on your thighs.

➡ THINNER THIGHS IN AN INSTANT

Here are several additional tricks for creating the illusion of thinner thighs:

- ☐ Wear thigh-flattering clothes. If your thighs are heavy, forget body-hugging knits such as mini skirts or leggings. Instead, wear soft, flowing skirts in flattering fabrics such as wool crepe or silk. These direct attention away from your thighs.

- ☐ Go neutral. Neutral colors cast a thin-thigh silhouette, so wear solid brown, navy blue, or black skirts. Avoid plaids, large patterns, or horizontal stripes.

- ☐ To make your legs look thin, always wear heels with the short-length dresses. Heels boost up the leg and buttock muscles, which can reduce the thigh fat and make them look thin, too.

- Apply leg makeup to make them look thin and long. Before applying makeup, wash the legs with body wash or soap and then apply a skin-toning product. This helps the makeup last longer.
- Use self-tanners. These lotions make legs look thin instantly. Plus, they hide flaws in skin such as dark spots, wrinkles, cellulite, or stretch marks.

Your thighs may never get as thin as a fashion model's, nor do you even want that stick-figure look. Continue watching your diet and exercising, and your thighs will get even more toned and strong. While you're working on your thighs, learn to take pleasure in the other parts of your body that are already to your liking. Then stay focused on being the best you that you can be.

7

PART 2
sexier in 7

Maybe you've heard the expression "Sexy is a state of mind." This to me is bullshit. Anyone who seriously believes this is either very deluded or else smoking some bad stuff. Just because someone thinks she's like Marilyn Monroe or Angelina Jolie doesn't make her either. You can't "state of mind" yourself into something you're not.

To my readers, I offer this advice: *Sexy is as sexy does.* Okay, neither Forrest Gump nor his mother ever said that, but sexy is not a state of mind. It's action: amping up your assets by staying in shape and taking care of yourself. That's what makes you sexy. To ooze sex, you've got to work it, baby, and work at it.

Here come my best look-sexy secrets. You may or may not agree with all of them, but hopefully you'll find something that grabs your attention and will give you some slammin' bod sexiness.

more beautiful eyes in 7

One of the biggest turn-ons to a guy is beautiful eyes. Innately, a man is drawn to a woman who is making eye contact with him. Your eyes are thus one of your most alluring assets—plus, they hold the rare distinction of being the window to the soul.

Over time though, eyes can lose their allure. You can get fine lines and crow's-feet, all usually caused by the same issue: loss of supportive collagen and elastin underneath the eye area. Or how about those dreaded dark circles? They're caused by an overproduction of melanin (a skin pigment), hormones, or dark broken blood vessels beneath the skin. Other causes are lack of sleep, an iron-deficient diet, fat loss beneath the eye, and bad habits like too much caffeine and tobacco.

And then there are those damn puffy underlids that make you look worn out. This area is very sensitive to swelling, so if you're retaining water, have allergies, or haven't gotten enough sleep, it's going to show up as puffy bags beneath the eyes. Also, as we age, the fat that protects the orbit of the eye comes out, creating the bump that we see beneath the eye.

My female patients constantly seek resolution to these problems, and certainly, I can deliver a number of cosmetic procedures to remedy them. I might do laser resurfacing or chemical peels to improve fine lines around the eyes. As skin heals, it tightens and stimulates the production of collagen. For dark circles, I use a laser called the Vbeam. It works by gently constricting and sealing the blood vessels that cause the purple-black color to appear through the skin. As for undereye bags, I use a relatively new procedure called *under-eye fat repositioning* that puts fat into the area where it's hollow and offers better results.

But before even considering those options, understand that a regular skincare routine for your eye area can improve fine lines, reduce crow's-feet, and ease dark circles and bags by up to 70 percent, as long as you stick with it.

I'll show you how, but first, for the next seven days and beyond, keep the following guidelines in mind for sexier eyes.

Give yourself ice cube massages. When I was the fight doctor (also called a *cutman*) for the boxer and five-time World Champion, Vinnie Paz, I was responsible for treating his injuries between rounds. When he had swelling under his eye, I'd iron out the area with a frozen piece of metal called an *en swell*. You can be your own cutman at home and iron out the swelling from around your eyes by gently massaging the area with an ice cube or frozen spoon. Essentially what you're doing is your own lymphatic massage and stimulating blood flow out of the eyes through the veins.

Avoid salt. For the next seven days, eliminate sodium from your diet. This means no table salt at meals and reading labels on everything you eat. (You'd be amazed at how much sodium is hidden in your favorite foods like canned soups, ketchup, and tomato sauce.) Meals may taste bland at first, but the improvement in your under-eye bags will be worth it. Use herbs and seasonings to spice up your food instead.

Curb the cocktails. Alcohol can have a dehydrating effect on your entire body, and your eye area is no exception. Dryness will make skin here look crepey, which highlights any fine lines. (Just think of how wrinkled a raisin is compared to a grape, and you'll get the idea.)

Alcohol can also disrupt your sleep, and without enough quality sleep, dark circles and under-eye bags can develop or worsen.

Get enough sleep. This is advice you've heard over and over—and we say it a lot on the show—but skimping on your sleep shows up on your face, in the form of sallow skin and puffy under-eye bags. (I guess that's why they call it "beauty sleep.") This week, count backward seven or eight hours from the time you have to get up in the morning to determine your bedtime. After seven days, not only will you look better, you'll feel more vibrant and energetic. Also, sleep with your head elevated on two pillows so fluid doesn't accumulate under the eyes while you sleep.

Hydrate, hydrate, hydrate. When skin is dry and dehydrated, any fine lines and wrinkles you have are more obvious. Because skin around the eyes has fewer oil glands than the rest of the face, it tends to get drier. Morning and night gently dot an eye cream with peptides or retinoids on the skin all around your eye. In addition to moisturizing, peptides and retinoids can boost the production of collagen, which thickens skin in that area. Over time this can improve under-eye darkness.

Use sunscreen daily. Most people forget the eye area when they're putting sunscreen on the face, or they are afraid to apply it here because the skin is too sensitive. The answer is finding a sunscreen made just for the eye area. If you can't, use one with physical sunblock ingredients like zinc oxide and titanium dioxide. Unlike chemical sunblocks that protect by absorbing into skin, these sit on the surface so they may be better for this fragile, easily irritated area.

Wear sunglasses any time you go out of the house. UV rays can increase your risk of cataracts and other vision problems, break down the thin skin around the eyes, and cause patches of pigmentation beneath them. Also, going without glasses on a sunny day means you're probably squinting, and this repetitive motion can etch fine little lines into your skin. Look for sunglasses with lenses that say they block 100 percent of UV rays. (Note: Pricey sunglasses are not necessarily better.)

Stop rubbing. For these seven days, take note of how often you're touching or rubbing your eyes. This kind of physical trauma can break down this delicate skin. It can also cause dark circles because the skin reacts to your rubbing as it would to an injury, stimulating your pigment cells as a result. You may also dilate blood vessels.

Take allergy medicine. Allergies not only can cause inflammation around the eyes but can dilate blood vessels beneath them. Because this area is so thin skinned, it's easy to see those blood vessels beneath the surface. Other symptoms include itchiness, runny nose, and redness. If you have allergies, try to keep them under control. Talk to your doctor about any allergy medications you can take.

Without further adieu, here's my recommended seven-day program for sexier eyes—and how it can help banish crow's-feet, puffiness, and dark circles through natural skincare technology and techniques.

Day 1

MORNING ROUTINE

When you wake up, sit quietly for three minutes with your eyes closed and take deep breaths counting to four on the inhale and exhale. This helps you de-stress—something that's important since dark circles can form if your body churns out too much cortisol, a stress hormone.

Sip my Eye Brightening Brew.

✚ DR. ORDON'S EYE BRIGHTENING BREW

INGREDIENTS:

- 4 to 5 green tea bags
- ½ small cucumber
- 1 lemon

INSTRUCTIONS:

Boil a pot of water. Let the tea bags steep in the hot water. Place the pot in the refrigerator to cool. Pour it into a pitcher and add eight slices of cucumber and the juice of the lemon. Drink one 8-ounce glass first thing in the morning and right before bed each night. This drink helps flush fluids and excess sodium from the body. Poor circulation can cause fluids to accumulate under your eyes causing bags and dark shadows.

If your eyes are puffy, use natural cool compresses on your eyes. I recommend a couple of options: tea compresses (see "Eye De-puffing Remedy"), cool cucumber slices that have been kept in the freezer, a small bag of frozen vegetables, or ice cubes or a frozen spoon placed over your eyes for 10 to 15 minutes. Any of these options will de-puff your eyes because cold constricts blood vessels and reduces swelling.

✚ DR. ORDON'S EYE DE-PUFFING REMEDY

INGREDIENTS:

- ☐ Caffeinated tea bag (any brand will do except for Earl Grey because it has an ingredient called oil of bergamot that can irritate delicate skin around the eyes)
- ☐ 1 cup of water
- ☐ Several cotton balls

INSTRUCTIONS:

Brew a cup of caffeinated tea. Let the tea cool. Soak cotton balls in it until they're saturated. Place the cotton balls in a plastic bag in the freezer for five to ten minutes.

For ten to fifteen minutes, lie with your head elevated on two pillows and cotton balls on your closed eyelids. Caffeine is a vasoconstrictor, so it helps to constrict blood vessels in this area, which remedies swelling and redness (and possibly some darkness), and the tannic acid in tea has an anti-inflammatory effect.

For dark circles, apply an eye cream containing hydroquinone, a lightening agent, around your eyes. Skin care products formulated for the eye area that contain vitamin K can also help. Alternatively, pat lemon juice–soaked cotton ball on the dark circles.

Apply an eye lid cream under your makeup that contains peptides and retinoids.

Next, apply a sun product made just for the eyes; this will protect against crow's-feet and other signs of aging. Physical blocks, like titanium dioxide, are the best.

Drink 1 cup of water while performing your morning routine. Staying well-hydrated can help prevent puffy eyes. Water keeps overall skin tone firm and full looking.

MID-MORNING
Drink 1 to 2 cups of water.

LUNCH
Drink 1 to 2 cups of water with lunch. Avoid salt.

MID-AFTERNOON
Snack on bananas and raisins, both of which alleviate bloating. Drink 1 to 2 cups of water.

DINNER
Drink 1 to 2 cups of water with dinner. Avoid alcohol; it causes dehydration.

EVENING ROUTINE
Sip a cup of my Eye Brightening Brew.

Gently remove eye makeup, using a mild makeup remover product or even baby wipes. Another option is to use olive oil, applied to a cotton ball. It helps nourish lashes and moisturizes the under-eye area.

Apply a moisturizing eye cream around the eye area. Consider the stretch-mark cream, StriVectin-SD. It helps diminish the appearance of fine lines, wrinkles, and crow's-feet. Tested in clinical trials, the anti-wrinkle peptide in this product turned out to be a key activating ingredient.

Apply and eyelash thickener conditioners like Talika Lipocils or Latisse, a prescription lash enhancer from Allergan.

Elevate your head while sleeping. It's not unusual to have puffy eyes after you get up in the morning. The reason is that after lying for hours in a horizontal position, you stand up, and the fluid that was resting under your eyes is suddenly being pulled down by gravity. This causes temporary swelling. To reduce it, elevate your head during sleep so that the fluid is not as drastically drawn down when you get up.

Day 2

MORNING ROUTINE
Do my three-minute deep-breathing exercise.

Sip my Eye Brightening Brew.

If your eyes are puffy, use natural cool compresses on your eyes.

For dark circles, apply an eye cream containing hydroquinone, a lightening agent, around your eyes, or an eye cream containing vitamin K. Alternatively, apply lemon juice on the dark circles.

Drink 1 cup of water while performing your morning routine.

MID-MORNING
Drink 1 to 2 cups of water.

LUNCH
Drink 1 to 2 cups of water with lunch. Avoid salt.

MID-AFTERNOON
Snack on bananas and raisins, both of which alleviate bloating. Drink 1 to 2 cups of water.

Exercise today for at least 30 minutes to improve circulation, which helps move fluid through your body, rather than letting it accumulate.

DINNER
Drink 1 to 2 cups of water with dinner. Avoid alcohol.

Sip a cup of my Eye Brightening Brew.

Gently remove eye makeup using a mild eye-makeup remover, baby wipes, or olive oil.

Apply a moisturizing eye cream around the eye area.

Apply your eyelash thickener and conditioner.

Elevate your head while sleeping.

Day 3

MORNING ROUTINE

Do my three-minute deep-breathing exercise.

Sip my Eye Brightening Brew.

If your eyes are puffy, use natural cool compresses on your eyes.

For dark circles, apply an eye cream containing hydroquinone, a lightening agent, around your eyes, or an eye cream containing vitamin K. Alternatively, apply lemon juice on the dark circles.

Drink 1 to 2 cups of water while performing your morning routine.

MID-MORNING

Drink 1 to 2 cups of water.

LUNCH

Drink 1 to 2 cups of water with lunch. Avoid salt.

MID-AFTERNOON

Drink 1 to 2 cups of water.

Have a special facial at a day spa, designed to treat and lift the skin around your eye.

DINNER

Drink 1 to 2 cups of water with dinner. Avoid alcohol.

EVENING ROUTINE

Sip my Eye Brightening Brew.

Gently remove eye makeup using a mild eye-makeup remover, baby wipes, or olive oil. Apply a moisturizing eye cream around the eye area.

Apply your eyelash thickener and conditioner.

Elevate your head while sleeping.

 # Day 4

MORNING ROUTINE
Do my three-minute deep-breathing exercise.

Sip my Eye Brightening Brew.

If your eyes are puffy, use natural cool compresses on your eyes.

For dark circles, apply an eye cream containing hydroquinone, or an eye cream containing vitamin K. Alternatively, apply lemon juice on the dark circles.

If dark circles continue to be a problem, switch to a cream containing niacinamide, a derivative of the vitamin niacin. It has been shown to be an effective skin-lightening agent, especially for skin conditions where excess pigmentation (hyperpigmentation) may occur on the face or other visible parts of the body. Look for a moisturizer containing 5 percent niacinamide.

Drink 1 to 2 cups of water while performing your morning routine.

MID-MORNING
Drink 1 to 2 cups of water.

LUNCH
Drink 1 to 2 cups of water with lunch. Avoid salt.

MID-AFTERNOON
Drink 1 to 2 cups of water.

Exercise today for at least 30 minutes.

DINNER
Drink 1 to 2 cups of water with dinner. Avoid alcohol.

Sip my Eye Brightening Brew.

Gently remove eye makeup using a mild eye-makeup remover, baby wipes, or olive oil.

Apply a moisturizing eye cream around the eye area.

Apply your eyelash thickener and conditioner.

Elevate your head while sleeping.

Day 5

MORNING ROUTINE
Do my three-minute deep-breathing exercise.

Sip my Eye Brightening Brew.

If your eyes are puffy, use natural cool compresses on your eyes.

For dark circles, apply an eye cream containing hydroquinone or an eye cream containing vitamin K. Alternatively, apply lemon juice on the dark circles. Or continue your niacinamide cream routine.

Drink 1 to 2 cups of water while performing your morning routine.

MID-MORNING
Drink 1 to 2 cups of water.

LUNCH
Drink 1 to 2 cups of water with lunch. Avoid salt.

MID-AFTERNOON
Drink 1 to 2 cups of water.

DINNER
Drink 1 to 2 cups of water with dinner. Avoid alcohol; it causes dehydration.

EVENING ROUTINE
Sip my Eye Brightening Brew.

Gently remove eye makeup using a mild eye-makeup remover, baby wipes, or olive oil.

Apply a moisturizing eye cream around the eye area.

Apply your eyelash thickener and conditioner.

Elevate your head while sleeping.

Day 6

MORNING ROUTINE

Do my three-minute deep-breathing exercise.

Sip my Eye Brightening Brew.

If your eyes are puffy, use natural cool compresses on your eyes.

For dark circles, apply an eye cream containing hydroquinone or an eye-makeup remover containing vitamin K. Alternatively, apply lemon juice on the dark circles. Or continue your niacinamide cream routine.

Drink 1 to 2 cups of water while performing your morning routine.

MID-MORNING

Drink 1 to 2 cups of water.

LUNCH

Drink 1 to 2 cups of water with lunch. Avoid salt.

MID-AFTERNOON

Drink 1 to 2 cups of water.

Exercise today for at least 30 minutes.

DINNER

Drink 1 to 2 cups of water with dinner. Avoid alcohol.

EVENING ROUTINE

Sip my Eye Brightening Brew.

Gently remove eye makeup using a mild eye-makeup remover, baby wipes, or olive oil.

Apply a moisturizing eye cream around the eye area.

Apply your eyelash thickener and conditioner.

Elevate your head while sleeping.

 # Day 7

MORNING ROUTINE

Do my three-minute deep-breathing exercise.

Sip my Eye Brightening Brew.

If your eyes are puffy, use natural cool compresses on your eyes.

For dark circles, apply an eye cream containing hydroquinone or an eye cream containing vitamin K. Alternatively, apply lemon juice on the dark circles. Or continue your niacinamide cream routine.

Drink 1 to 2 cups of water while performing your morning routine.

MID-MORNING

Drink 1 to 2 cups of water.

LUNCH

Drink 1 to 2 cups of water with lunch. Avoid salt.

MID-AFTERNOON

Drink 1 to 2 cups of water.

DINNER

Drink 1 to 2 cups of water with dinner. Avoid alcohol.

EVENING ROUTINE

Sip my Eye Brightening Brew.

Gently remove eye makeup using a mild eye-makeup remover, baby wipes or olive oil.

Apply a moisturizing eye cream around the eye area.

Apply your eyelash thickener and conditioner.

Elevate your head while sleeping.

One of the sexiest beauty assets you can flaunt are your eyes. Follow this routine faithfully, and you'll sex up your looks in no time.

➡ MAKEUP TRICKS FOR SEXY EYES

Make your eyes look better today with these tips I learned from one of the makeup artists on the set:

☐ **After you've applied your foundation, apply an eye makeup primer to your eyelid, from your lashes all the way to your brow line.** Make sure you have a smooth base.

☐ **Using a small brush, cover your upper lids and just below your brow line with a shimmery, taupe or cream-colored eye shadow.** The sparkle helps brighten your eyes and draws attention upward.

☐ **Consider false eyelashes.** There are many brands on the market, but my patients like the lashes made by Ardell. They look the most natural, and you can buy them in any pharmacy or mass-market chain. Use a clear glue, and apply it to the back of the lash. Leave it to dry for 15 to 30 seconds for better adhesion. (If you let the glue set first, the lashes won't slip around.) Next, hold the lash with some tweezers, look down and place the lash into the middle of your eye, tucking each side in and then pressing down so it sticks.

☐ **Lash it up.** Use a volumizing mascara on your top and bottom lashes (yes, even over the false lashes) to emphasize the eyes and create lovely long lashes. If you opt out of using false eyelashes, curl your upper lashes with a lash curler. This alone gives the appearance of bigger, brighter lashes and diverts attention from under-eye problems.

☐ **With a slanted eye-makeup brush, apply a dark smoky shade of brown** to the far corner of your eye, making a little triangle.

☐ **Add definition to your eyes by contouring your socket with a sweep of taupe across the crease of your lid,** flicking outward rather than down, to open and extend the eye.

☐ **Dip a small, firm, fine-pointed eyeliner brush in a good smudge-proof liner.** Gently pull the skin of your brow to ensure your eyelid is taught, steadily drawing a fine line as close to your lashes as possible; start from the inner corner and slowly trace outward in one smooth movement. Line your lower lids too, but smudge the liner slightly.

- **Camouflage dark circles and puffiness.** Purchase a concealer that is one to two shades lighter than your normal foundation. (Yellow concealers work well for lighter skin, and an orange tone works best for darker skin.) Over your foundation, apply the concealer to the under-eye lid area, in a large half-moon shape, beginning from just under the tear ducts arcing up to your temples. Blend the concealer into your foundation, and powder the area with a translucent powder to even out the color. Smooth over fine lines and imperfections.

- **Define your brows.** People always forget about their eyebrows, but making yours look neat and tidy finishes off the look. Use a powder-based product to give some definition to your brows. To line your brows perfectly, place one end of a pen or pencil vertically at the outside edge of one nostril and extend it straight up to the brow area. This is where the brow should start. To find the middle, the highest part of the arch, place the pencil at the tip of the nostril, then line it up with the iris of your eye. The end of the brow should be at the outer corner of your eyes. Slightly extend the beginning of your brows so that they look closer to your eyes. The most beautiful women in the world have eyebrows that, at their beginning, are set very close to their inner eyelids. You can accomplish this easily with brow liner.

  Eyebrow guru Anastasia Soare, a woman whose been taming and shaping the brows of celebrities and other woman for more than 20 years, has been on our show a couple of times. I asked her the biggest mistake women make with brows, and she said it was over-tweezing. Not only do thin, short brows make your eyes look smaller, but you can actually damage your hair follicles in the brow area so hairs don't grow back. Err on the side of tweezing less, not more.

ASK DR. O

Can tugging at your eyes while applying eye makeup or putting in contact lenses cause wrinkles?

Yes. Over the long term, any external physical trauma, from rubbing your eyes to strong wind, can damage the delicate skin around your eyes. That said, you can still apply makeup and put in your lenses. Just make sure to use a very gentle hand and apply creams or makeup with your ring finger, which is the weakest so it gives the lightest touch. Also, wear protective eye gear when you're outdoors.

 SEE YOUR M.D. ASAP

Several underlying medical conditions can cause under-eye bags, so if yours don't improve after these seven days, you may want to see your doctor. These conditions include allergies, an overactive thyroid, diminished kidney function, and congestive heart failure. These would all be accompanied by other symptoms besides puffiness, but if you're concerned, see your doctor.

FACT OR FICTION?

Preparation H can deflate under-eye bags.

Using this hemorrhoid cream beneath the eyes is an old Hollywood recipe for reducing puffiness, and it may provide temporary relief. Preparation H is a vasoconstrictor, so it constricts the blood vessels, and because the skin is so thin, you may get some improvement. That said, the results are temporary, there are other ingredients in Preparation H that can potentially irritate sensitive skin, and this is one product you don't want to get in your eye.

a better smile in 7

Ladies, there's one thing that will make a guy go gaga over you, and it's not your boobs, a tight ass, or legs that go on for days. It's your smile. That's right—your smile. Men won't even approach you if your smile isn't genuine. A great smile is a true man magnet.

Need proof? A survey conducted by the American Dental Association and Crest and Oral B asked the following question: What do people find most attractive in others? Well, the answer was: a smile. It outranked eyes, hair, and body when it comes to the most attractive physical feature.

Not only does a smile make you more attractive, it makes you appear more confident, generates trust, and makes you more successful in life. Your smile is the secret for success in just about every part of life.

Okay, so maybe you're thinking your mouth area isn't worth smiling about. Let's talk about how to look after your smile, from lips to teeth and more. I believe taking care of your smile must be an essential part of your daily routine, not just for looking good but for overall general health. My seven-day program includes the following:

Teeth Whitening

White teeth, for example, indicate good health and vitality, which is a key trait guys subconsciously zero in on when they're checking out the opposite sex. Most whitening treatments use hydrogen peroxide—the same stuff used to bleach hair—or carbamide peroxide (a more viscous, easier-to-handle form of hydrogen peroxide) to lighten stains.

There are many methods of bleaching. I'll give you some of the quickest, cheapest, and most effective methods in my seven-day plan. But first, I'd be remiss if I didn't mention that routinely drinking liquids that stain tooth enamel (coffee and red wine, for example) will dull the effect more quickly, so drink this stuff with a straw. It might look stupid, but who cares? You're improving your looks, and it's no one's business that you're slurping to do it.

Dental Care

Your teeth are at the heart of your smile. If they look nice, you have sex appeal, period. A clean, attractive mouth also helps your sense of well-being, self-esteem, and pride in your appearance. Proper brushing twice a day and flossing daily helps prevent periodontal disease. And be sure to get a professional cleaning every three to six months by a dentist or dental hygienist in order to remove plaque from areas that might otherwise be susceptible to periodontal disease.

Lip Exfoliation

Exfoliating your lips gets rid of dry, dull skin and instantly makes lips look plumper and pinker. You don't need to buy expensive lip exfoliation creams. You can make the following exfoliator in minutes with ingredients you've got at home. Afterward, try my Tropical Lip Balm for soft, super-kissable lips.

✚ DR. ORDON'S QUICK AND EASY LIP EXFOLIATION CREAM

In a small bowl, combine the following:

- ½ teaspoon moisturizing lotion (such as Oil of Olay's Active Hydrating Body Fluid)
- ¼ teaspoon fresh coffee grounds
- ¼ teaspoon Kosher salt

Mix well. Apply to entire mouth area and massage around for about five minutes. Wipe clean with a warm wet washcloth. Apply my Tropical Lip Balm to your lips.

✚ DR. ORDON'S TROPICAL LIP BALM

In a small bowl, combine the following:

- 1 tablespoon of petroleum jelly with cocoa butter (such as Vaseline)
- ½ teaspoon of liquid coconut oil
- Contents of 2 vitamin E capsules

Mix well and store in a tiny container or empty lip balm container. Apply to your lips after exfoliating or any time to moisturize.

Fuller Lips

Lips thin with age, and this can detract from your looks. The easiest fix is with makeup: Coat your lips with foundation, and let it dry. Use a lip liner that is about two shades darker than your lips. Define the outline of your lips, just along the borders and not above. Blend in the edges with a lip brush so there are no harsh edges. Apply another layer of foundation. Apply a neutral frosty lip color such as pinky beige; it makes your mouth appear fuller. Dab a touch of lip gloss in a similar shade, but just at the center of your top of bottom lips, to get a wet pouty look. It'll highlight your smile and enhance the shape of your mouth.

You can also try lip plumpers. Most of these products contain mild irritants that cause the blood to rush to the surface of the lips, which flushes and swells them slightly. Other products are formulated with special fats that attract moisture from inside the lip and inflate to plump up the lips. The effect of these products is not permanent; you must continually apply it throughout the day, or before you apply your lipstick.

Now for my seven-day plan.

Day 1

MORNING ROUTINE

After breakfast, rinse your mouth with a whitening mouthwash, such as Listerine Whitening Vibrant White Pre-Brush Rinse.

Brush your teeth using my Whitening Toothpaste (see "Dr. Ordon's Whitening Toothpaste"). In a week or two, your bright white teeth will gradually emerge!

Floss.

Exfoliate your lips with my Quick and Easy Lip Exfoliation Cream.

Apply your makeup, using my techniques for fuller lips.

✚ DR. ORDON'S WHITENING TOOTHPASTE

Brush your teeth using the following formula: Mix a half a capful of hydrogen peroxide and half a tablespoon of baking soda. This is a highly effective home remedy for perfect white teeth and should be used twice a day for a week. Baking soda is a mild abrasive and is very effective in maintaining white teeth.

LUNCHTIME

Choose crunchy fruits and veggies, such as apple slices, carrots, and celery sticks. They actually help clean your teeth while you munch.

AFTER LUNCH

Chew whitening sugar-free gum; it can absorb some of the new-to-the-surface stains when you don't have time to brush.

EVENING ROUTINE

After dinner, swish water around in your mouth to eliminate any remaining food particles.

Wash your mouth with a whitening mouthwash, such as Listerine Whitening Vibrant White Pre-Brush Rinse.

Brush your teeth with my Whitening Toothpaste.

Floss.

Exfoliate your lips with my Quick and Easy Lip Exfoliation Cream.

Apply my Tropical Lip Balm liberally to your lips.

 Day 2

MORNING ROUTINE

Wash your mouth with a prebrush whitening mouthwash.

Brush your teeth with my Whitening Toothpaste.

Floss.

Exfoliate your lips with my Quick and Easy Lip Exfoliation Cream.

Apply your makeup, using my techniques for fuller lips.

Wear a product such as Crest White Strips across your teeth. Leave them on for 30 minutes.

LUNCHTIME

Choose crunchy fruits and veggies, such as apple slices, carrots, and celery sticks.

AFTER LUNCH
Chew whitening sugar-free gum.

EVENING ROUTINE
After dinner, swish water around in your mouth to eliminate any remaining food particles.

Wear a product such as Crest White Strips across your teeth. Leave them on for 30 minutes.

Wash your mouth with a prebrush whitening mouthwash.

Brush your teeth with my Whitening Toothpaste.

Floss.

Exfoliate your lips with my Quick and Easy Lip Exfoliation Cream.

Apply my Tropical Lip Balm liberally to your lips.

Day 3

MORNING ROUTINE
After breakfast, wash your mouth with a prebrush whitening mouthwash.

Brush your teeth with my Whitening Toothpaste.

Floss.

Exfoliate your lips with my Quick and Easy Lip Exfoliation Cream.

Apply your makeup, using my techniques for fuller lips.

LUNCHTIME
Choose crunchy fruits and veggies, such as apple slices, carrots, and celery sticks.

AFTER LUNCH
Chew whitening sugar-free gum.

EVENING ROUTINE
After dinner, swish water around in your mouth to eliminate any remaining food particles.

AT BEDTIME

Wash your mouth with a prebrush whitening mouthwash.

Brush your teeth with my Whitening Toothpaste.

Floss.

Exfoliate your lips with my Quick and Easy Lip Exfoliation Cream.

Apply my Tropical Lip Balm liberally to your lips.

Day 4

MORNING ROUTINE

Wash your mouth with a whitening mouthwash, such as Listerine Whitening Vibrant White Pre-Brush Rinse.

Brush your teeth with my Whitening Toothpaste.

Floss.

Exfoliate your lips with my Quick and Easy Lip Exfoliation Cream.

Apply your makeup, using my techniques for fuller lips.

Wear a product such as Crest White Strips across your teeth. Leave them on for 30 minutes.

LUNCHTIME

Choose crunchy fruits and veggies, such as apple slices, carrots, and celery sticks.

AFTER LUNCH

Chew whitening sugar-free gum.

AFTER DINNER

Swish water around in your mouth to eliminate any remaining food particles.

Wear a product such as Crest White Strips across your teeth. Leave them on for 30 minutes.

AT BEDTIME

Wash your mouth with a whitening mouthwash, such as Listerine Whitening Vibrant White Pre-Brush Rinse.

Brush your teeth with my Whitening Toothpaste.

Floss.

Exfoliate your lips with my Quick and Easy Lip Exfoliation Cream.

Apply my Tropical Lip Balm liberally to your lips.

Day 5

MORNING ROUTINE

Wash your mouth with a whitening mouthwash, such as Listerine Whitening Vibrant White Pre-Brush Rinse.

Brush your teeth with my Whitening Toothpaste.

Floss.

Exfoliate your lips with my Quick and Easy Lip Exfoliation Cream.

Apply your makeup, using my techniques for fuller lips.

LUNCHTIME

Choose crunchy fruits and veggies, such as apple slices, carrots, and celery sticks.

AFTER LUNCH

Chew whitening sugar-free gum.

AFTER DINNER

Swish water around in your mouth to eliminate any remaining food particles.

AT BEDTIME

Wash your mouth with a whitening mouthwash.

Brush your teeth with my Whitening Toothpaste.

Floss.

Exfoliate your lips with my Quick and Easy Lip Exfoliation Cream.

Apply my Tropical Lip Balm liberally to your lips.

Day 6

MORNING ROUTINE

Wash your mouth with a whitening mouthwash.

Brush your teeth with my Whitening Toothpaste.

Floss.

Exfoliate your lips with my Quick and Easy Lip Exfoliation Cream.

Apply your makeup, using my techniques for fuller lips.

Wear a product such as Crest White Strips across your teeth. Leave them on for 30 minutes.

LUNCHTIME

Choose crunchy fruits and veggies, such as apple slices, carrots, and celery sticks.

AFTER LUNCH

Chew whitening sugar-free gum.

AFTER DINNER

Swish water around in your mouth to eliminate any remaining food particles.

Wear a product such as Crest White Strips across your teeth. Leave them on for 30 minutes.

AT BEDTIME

Wash your mouth with a whitening mouthwash.

Brush your teeth with my Whitening Toothpaste.

Floss.

Exfoliate your lips with my Quick and Easy Lip Exfoliation Cream.

Apply my Tropical Lip Balm liberally to your lips.

Day 7

MORNING ROUTINE

Wash your mouth with a whitening mouthwash.

Brush your teeth with my Whitening Toothpaste.

Floss.

Exfoliate your lips with my Quick and Easy Lip Exfoliation Cream.

Apply your makeup, using my techniques for fuller lips.

LUNCHTIME

Choose crunchy fruits and veggies, such as apple slices, carrots, and celery sticks.

AFTER LUNCH

Chew whitening sugar-free gum.

AFTER DINNER

Swish water around in your mouth to eliminate any remaining food particles.

AT BEDTIME

Wash your mouth with a whitening mouthwash.

Brush your teeth with my Whitening Toothpaste.

Floss.

Exfoliate your lips with my Quick and Easy Lip Exfoliation Cream.

Apply my Tropical Lip Balm liberally to your lips.

Finally, adopt the smile habit: Ladies, please practice this in front of your mirror. Smile! Smile! Smile!

less cellulite in 7

Look at your thighs, and you'll probably notice *cellulite*, that lumpy-looking puckered skin that resembles a plate of cottage cheese just under your skin. If you have it—and chances are you do—the question is, can you get rid of it?

Women ask me this all the time. They've heard that you can't, that it's hopeless to try. Not true—there is much you can to do minimize it and even make your body cellulite-resistant in the future. All it takes is a willingness to try and the commitment to stay at it.

So, what is this imperfection called cellulite? For starters, it's not a disease or a medical problem but rather an unsexy fat that has "gone wild." It's located in the uppermost layer of subcutaneous (under the skin) fat. This layer is structurally compartmentalized in tiny upright chambers arched like church windows. These chambers are framed with connective tissue. In women, these fat chambers can increase up to 300 times their normal size. When this happens, too much fat gets crammed inside. The overstuffed chambers make the skin jut out, creating that all-too-familiar quilt-like appearance we know as cellulite.

What causes cellulite? We don't know for sure, but it's a probable combination of the following factors:

- Estrogen, which causes the body to store fat and break down connective tissue
- Water retention
- Poor circulation
- Faulty lymphatic circulation and drainage
- The buildup of toxins in the body
- Fat gain
- Aging
- Genetics
- Lifestyle factors, such as poor diet, lack of exercise, and overexposure to sun

The Exercise Solution

I will add here that the very best natural solution for minimizing cellulite and making your body cellulite-resistant is exercising, specifically strength and flexibility moves. So, if you have cellulite, stop the exercise excuses, get off your butt, and start moving.

Tightening the muscles under your skin makes cellulite less pronounced, which is why I recommend regular strength training. Strength training fights cellulite in a couple of important ways. First, it improves blood and lymph circulation. Exercising the lower body (where cellulite congregates) forces the leg muscles to contract—an action that pushes venous blood and lymph fluid back toward the heart, improving overall circulation. Second, strength training increases the size and tone of your leg muscles and, in doing so, irons out cellulite, thus improving overall skin tone.

It's also critical to work your connective tissue so that it stays flexible. Flexible connective tissue retains its elasticity, an important component of a cellulite-free body. Stretching is the best way to gain and preserve flexibility.

I favor combining strength and flexibility work through a method of stretching between exercise sets. When you stretch between sets, you expand a type of connective tissue called the *fascia*, which envelops the muscle. With the fascia expanded, the muscle has more room to grow and develop. The greater your muscle development, the less cellulite you have, and the more cellulite resistant your body becomes. As part of my seven-day program, you'll do the following exercises and stretches.

DUMBBELL SQUAT

Hold a dumbbell in each hand alongside your body, and stand with your feet a comfortable distance apart. Keeping your back straight, squat down until your thighs are just lower than parallel to the floor. Return to the starting position, and repeat the exercise as many times as you can. Try to keep constant tension on your thighs and buttocks as you perform this exercise.

THIGH STRETCH

Stand next to a sturdy chair. Bend your left knee. Holding your left ankle, bring your bent leg behind you. For balance, hold on to the chair. Press your left heel to your buttocks, while pushing your thigh down and back. Hold for 10 to 20 seconds, then release. Repeat with your right thigh.

WALKING DUMBBELL LUNGES

These are an excellent shaping and toning exercise for your thighs and hips. For this exercise, you'll need a large area such as a track or a spacious room. To begin, hold a dumbbell in each hand at your sides. While keeping your back straight, step forward on your right leg as far as possible until your right thigh is parallel to the floor. Try to hold your left leg as straight as possible. Repeat this movement with your left leg. Continue to step forward in this fashion for a full five minutes.

STRAIGHT-LEG DEADLIFT WITH DUMBBELLS

Start with two dumbbells on the floor (about 8 to 12 pounds each). Take a shoulder-width stance. Grasp both weights by curling your hands over the dumbbells.

Next, bend over the dumbbells, keeping your back flat, knees bent, and head up. Without bending your arms, lift the weights up from the floor until your body is perfectly upright. Lower the dumbbells and repeat the exercise. Concentrate on using the strength of your legs and hips throughout the exercise.

BUTTERFLY STRETCH

This movement stretches your inner thighs and hips. Sit on the floor with your knees bent and apart and the bottoms of your feet pressed together. With your back arched slightly, move your upper body forward while pressing your inner thighs down toward the floor. Hold for a count of 10 to 20 seconds.

SIDE LUNGE

Hold a dumbbell in each hand at your sides. Keeping your back as straight as possible, step out to your right side as far as you can until your thigh is just about parallel to the floor. Try to keep your left leg straight. Step back to the starting position and continue the exercise on your right leg for the suggested number of repetitions. Repeat the exercise with your left leg.

INNER THIGH/HAMSTRING STRETCH

Sit on the floor with your legs spread as wide apart as possible. Press your upper body toward the floor as you walk forward with your hands as far as you can. Hold for a count of 10 to 20 seconds; then release.

If you're battling cellulite, you're definitely not alone. Most women have cellulite, from supermodels to the very obese. But that doesn't mean you can't do something about it. Here's my seven-day plan to help you get that process underway.

 Day 1

MORNING ROUTINE

Every morning, drink a glass of hot water with lemon; the effect of the lemon combined with hot water helps detox your body.

WITH BREAKFAST

Take 1,000 milligrams of supplemental vitamin C. It improves circulation and assists the body in synthesizing collagen—two actions that help minimize cellulite.

EVERY TWO TO THREE HOURS

Drink 1 cup of water. Water keeps your metabolism going and circulation flowing and prevents the collection of fat.

TWICE A DAY

Apply a product called Oligo.DX Cellulite Reducing Gel to cellulite-affected areas. This product contains caffeine and a flavonoid-rich Nelumbo nucifera extract (made from the seeds of the lotus). In research, it reduced cellulite significantly for 89 percent of women who used it.

TODAY'S WORKOUT

EXERCISE/STRETCH	SETS	REPETITIONS
Dumbbell Squat	Warm-up set (no weight)	10 to 12
	2—increase poundage each set	12 to 15
Thigh Stretch	3—perform between dumbbell squat sets	Hold stretch 10 to 20 seconds
Walking Dumbbell Lunges	Walk/lunge for 5 minutes	As many as possible
Thigh Stretch	3—perform between walking dumbbell lunges	Hold stretch 10 to 20 seconds
Straight-Leg Deadlift with Dumbbells	Warm-up set (no weight)	10 to 12
	2—increase poundage each set	12 to 15
Butterfly Stretch	3—perform between Straight-Leg Deadlifts	Hold stretch 10 to 20 seconds
Side Lunge	1	12 to 15 each leg
Inner Thigh/ Hamstring Stretch	1—performed after Side Lunges	Hold stretch 10 to 20 seconds

Get rid of—and stop eating—added sugar of any kind (table sugar, honey, syrup, or brown sugar). An excess of sugary foods can suppress blood flow to fatty tissue. Reduced blood flow prevents fat from being burned. Sugar also speeds up age-related changes in collagen, the connective tissue that keeps skin tight. Basically, sugar rushing into the bloodstream as glucose causes collagen to "cross link," an undesirable process in which collagen molecules bind chemically to each other. Cross-linking damages elasticity in the skin and degrades collagen—two problems that aggravate cellulite. So, avoid sugar if you're fighting cellulite.

 # Day 2

MORNING ROUTINE
Drink a glass of hot water with lemon.

WITH BREAKFAST
Take 1,000 milligrams of supplemental vitamin C.

EVERY TWO TO THREE HOURS
Drink 1 cup of water.

TWICE A DAY
Apply Oligo.DX Cellulite Reducing Gel to cellulite-affected areas.

TODAY'S WORKOUT: ANTI-CELLULITE
WORKOUT (CARDIOVASCULAR)
Cardiovascular exercise—the kind that gets your heart pumping—helps minimize cellulite, for two main reasons. It deflabs your body and enhances blood circulation. As I mentioned earlier, fat gain and poor circulation contribute to cellulite. So, cardiovascular exercise attacks cellulite on both fronts.

There are lots of cardiovascular exercises you can choose; they're all effective—biking, indoor exercise machines, aerobics dance classes, the whole gambit. But if you can start a brisk walking program and progress to jogging and running, do it. I've rarely seen a woman runner who has cellulite!

Today, I want you to do 45 to 60 minutes of cardiovascular activity, even if it's just walking.

EVENING ROUTINE

Prepare and apply my Anti-Cellulite Seaweed Wrap (see instructions).

✚ DR. ORDON'S ANTI-CELLULITE SEAWEED WRAP*

Exfoliate your skin with a loofah, warm water, and soap to remove the dead skin from the top layer of your skin.

Prepare the wrap:

- ☐ Pour ½ cup of seaweed powder into a mixing bowl. Seaweed powder is readily available at most health food stores or online.
- ☐ Add a bit of water until the mixture forms a paste.
- ☐ Drizzle in ¼ cup of baby oil. Add four drops of lavender oil, if desired. Mix well.

Sit in the bathtub and gently massage the seaweed mixture into your skin. Work from your ankles to the tops and backs of your thighs.

Cover each leg firmly with plastic wrap. Lie still for 30 minutes.

Carefully unwrap your legs and rinse off with warm water.

Use this wrap any time prior to going out with bare legs.

ADDITIONAL ACTIONS

Begin "dry skin brushing" today. This technique stimulates blood and lymph circulation to cellulite-affected areas, plus improves skin texture and appearance. With a small, stiff brush or massage glove, brush from your feet upward in long strokes all over your body toward the heart. Use gentle strokes, and avoid brushing over any skin wounds or sores. Brush every day for 5 to 10 minutes.

■ Day 3

MORNING ROUTINE
Drink a glass of hot water with lemon.

WITH BREAKFAST
Take 1,000 milligrams of supplemental vitamin C.

EVERY TWO TO THREE HOURS
Drink 1 cup of water.

TWICE A DAY
Apply Oligo.DX Cellulite Reducing Gel to cellulite-affected areas.

TODAY'S WORKOUT

EXERCISE/STRETCH	SETS	REPETITIONS
Dumbbell Squat	Warm-up set (no weight)	10 to 12
	2—increase poundage each set	12 to 15
Thigh Stretch	3—perform between dumbbell squat sets	Hold stretch 10 to 20 seconds
Walking Dumbbell Lunges	Walk/lunge for 5 minutes	As many as possible
Thigh Stretch	3—perform between walking dumbbell lunges	Hold stretch 10 to 20 seconds
Straight-Leg Deadlift with Dumbbells	Warm-up set (no weight)	10 to 12
	2—increase poundage each set	12 to 15
Butterfly Stretch	3—perform between Straight-Leg Deadlifts	Hold stretch 10 to 20 seconds
Side Lunge	1	12- to 15 each leg
Inner Thigh/ Hamstring Stretch	1—performed after Side Lunges	Hold stretch 10 to 20 seconds

Bump up the fiber in your diet by eating more fruits and vegetables daily. Fiber is a cellulite fighter. It grabs toxins and clears them out quickly. Speedy waste clearing will leave you with a flatter stomach, clearer skin, and less cellulite. All plant foods contain fiber, but the best sources are apples, pears, berries, beans, corn, peas, bran, and high-fiber cold cereals. I suggest that you take in around 35 grams of fiber a day.

Day 4

MORNING ROUTINE
Drink a glass of hot water with lemon.

WITH BREAKFAST
Take 1,000 milligrams of supplemental vitamin C.

EVERY TWO TO THREE HOURS
Drink 1 cup of water.

TWICE A DAY
Apply Oligo.DX Cellulite Reducing Gel to cellulite-affected areas.

TODAY'S WORKOUT: ANTI-CELLULITE WORKOUT (AEROBICS)
Perform 45 to 60 minutes of cardiovascular activity, even if it's just walking.

EVENING ROUTINE
Prepare and apply my Anti-Cellulite Seaweed Wrap (see instructions on page 77).

Camouflage your cellulite. Invest in some spray-on leg makeup. It's just an optical illusion but one that can help make your legs look slimmer and cellulite free. Spray the product on your legs very lightly, and then rub it in to distribute the makeup evenly. Sally Hansen Airbrush Legs (waterproof) is good, but there are lots of these products on the market. Experiment. You'll be surprised how well they mask cellulite, plus make your legs look youthful.

📅 Day 5

MORNING ROUTINE
Every morning, drink a glass of hot water with lemon.

WITH BREAKFAST
Take 1,000 milligrams of supplemental vitamin C.

EVERY TWO TO THREE HOURS
Drink 1 cup of water.

TWICE A DAY
Apply Oligo.DX Cellulite Reducing Gel to cellulite–affected areas.

TODAY'S WORKOUT

EXERCISE/STRETCH	SETS	REPETITIONS
Dumbbell Squat	Warm-up set (no weight)	10 to 12
	2—increase poundage each set	12 to 15
Thigh Stretch	3—perform between dumbbell squat sets	Hold stretch 10 to 20 seconds
Walking Dumbbell Lunges	Walk/lunge for 5 minutes	As many as possible
Thigh Stretch	3—perform between walking dumbbell lunges	Hold stretch 10 to 20 seconds
Straight-Leg Deadlift with Dumbbells	Warm-up set (no weight)	10 to 12
	2—increase poundage each set	12 to 15
Butterfly Stretch	3—perform between Straight-Leg Deadlifts	Hold stretch 10 to 20 seconds
Side Lunge	1	12- to 15 each leg
Inner Thigh/ Hamstring Stretch	1—performed after Side Lunges	Hold stretch 10 to 20 seconds

Another way to camouflage cellulite is with a self-tanner. These work by causing a protein reaction in the skin that dyes only your surface cells. These lotions are likely to contain moisturizers, so the texture of your skin could also improve.

Remove dead layers of skin by exfoliating with a loofah. Apply a small amount of the tanner every other day, so you can see and correct mistakes in between. For trouble spots such as ankles, wrists, hands, and knees, add a dab of moisturizer rubbed in on top of the tanner to blend the color better.

Day 6

MORNING ROUTINE
Drink a glass of hot water with lemon.

WITH BREAKFAST
Take 1,000 milligrams of supplemental vitamin C.

EVERY TWO TO THREE HOURS
Drink 1 cup of water.

TWICE A DAY
Apply Oligo.DX Cellulite Reducing Gel to cellulite-affected areas.

TODAY'S WORKOUT
Perform 45 to 60 minutes of cardiovascular activity, even if it's just walking.

EVENING ROUTINE
Prepare and apply my Anti-Cellulite Seaweed Wrap (see instructions on page 77).

On *The Doctors*, I featured some French-made jeans designed to fight cellulite. Inside the fabric are micro-encapsulated active ingredients, including green tea. It may really decrease your cellulite, at least temporarily, because of the caffeine found in green tea. You have to wear the jeans for around 28 days, though, to see some benefits, and you can't wash them during that time. Because caffeine exerts some positive action against cellulite, you may want to check into this "wearable treatment" as part of your overall cellulite-fighting plan.

 Day 7

MORNING ROUTINE
Drink a glass of hot water with lemon.

WITH BREAKFAST
Take 1,000 milligrams of supplemental vitamin C.

EVERY TWO TO THREE HOURS
Drink 1 cup of water.

TWICE A DAY
Apply Oligo.DX Cellulite Reducing Gel to cellulite-affected areas.

TODAY'S WORKOUT

EXERCISE/STRETCH	SETS	REPETITIONS
Dumbbell Squat	Warm-up set (no weight)	10 to 12
	2—increase poundage each set	12 to 15
Thigh Stretch	3—perform between dumbbell squat sets	Hold stretch 10 to 20 seconds
Walking Dumbbell Lunges	Walk/lunge for 5 minutes	As many as possible
Thigh Stretch	3—perform between walking dumbbell lunges	Hold stretch 10 to 20 seconds

EXERCISE/STRETCH	SETS	REPETITIONS
Straight-Leg Deadlift with Dumbbells	Warm-up set (no weight)	10 to 12
	2—increase poundage each set	12 to 15
Butterfly Stretch	3—perform between Straight-Leg Deadlifts	Hold stretch 10 to 20 seconds
Side Lunge	1	12- to 15 each leg
Inner Thigh/ Hamstring Stretch	1—performed after Side Lunges	Hold stretch 10 to 20 seconds

ADDITIONAL ACTIONS

Add to your lifestyle activities that relieve stress—yoga, meditation, counseling, relaxation exercises, and so forth. Stress churns out the hormone insulin. Insulin promotes fat storage, providing more places for cellulite dimples to lurk.

➡ 7 FACTORS THAT MAKE CELLULITE WORSE

1. **Drinking alcohol.** Alcohol dehydrates the body and destroys B vitamins, which keep your skin elastic and smooth.

2. **Smoking.** This worst-of-all bad habits interferes with the body's use of vitamin C. You need vitamin C to make skin-strengthening collagen and to keep your body cellulite resistant.

3. **Salting foods.** Salt causes water retention and makes your skin look puffy.

4. **Eating processed foods.** Highly refined foods are loaded with salt and sugar—two additives that aggravate cellulite.

5. **Yo-yo dieting.** Going off and on diets promotes the development of cellulite. Women who repeatedly yo-yo diet tend to have higher deposits of fat on their hips and buttocks than those who keep their weight fairly stable.

6. **Sunbathing.** Repeated exposure to sun increases the activity of

tissue-damaging free radicals. Free radical damage promotes the formation of an abnormal type of collagen—one that is quite inelastic. Your skin gets looser and less elastic, and cellulite becomes more obvious.

7. **Not exercising regularly.** Women who don't exercise tend to be heavier, with more cellulite, than women who work out regularly.

There's Hope

The development of cellulite can't yet be traced to a single cause; multiple factors are at work. But if you look at the causes of cellulite that I listed earlier, you'll see that, with the exception of aging and genetic factors, most are controllable. I hope that encourages you. With better personal care, the proper natural treatments, and positive changes in your lifestyle, you can prevent cellulite, minimize its appearance, and stop its progression altogether.

reduce stretch marks in 7

If have a growth spurt, get pregnant, or gain a lot of weight fast, expect to develop lines on your body called *stretch marks*. They're basically scars that form when underlying skin tissue is overstretched by rapid growth. This sort of assault disrupts the normal production of collagen, the major protein in connective tissue in your skin.

If you have stretch marks, you're not alone. Stretch marks are about two and half times as frequent in women and affect 70 to 90 percent of pregnant women. They first appear in a pinkish or purple-ish color but will soon fade into a grayish white with time. I don't think you should be too ashamed of them; they show you've lived and represent the wonderful experience of giving birth. Still, to many women, they're cosmetically troublesome, and not sexy, especially when you have to wear a bathing suit or shorts.

Although I treat stretch marks through lasers, dermabrasion, or chemical peels, I have recommended other less rigorous options to minimize them. The following are some examples.

Topical Treatments

Hundreds of topical products are available in the market, but no one has ever proved they make a difference. One exception is a product called Trofolastin, a cream that contains collagen-elastin derivative, vitamin E, and extracts of Centella asiatica (from the herb gotu kola), which is believed to be the key therapeutic substance that fights stretch marks.

Studies have shown that regular application of this product can prevent the development of stretch marks, which is why this formula is often recommended to pregnant women. The popular stretch mark cream Mederma also contains Centella asiatica.

Other lotions marketed as stretch mark treatments typically contain alpha hydroxy acid (AHA) formulations. AHA helps strip off the top layer of skin cells, allowing newer, healthier skin cells to emerge. This action also lets moisturizers penetrate the skin more deeply, for smoother, softer skin.

Massaging certain natural oils into the skin will also improve the elasticity and reduce the appearance of stretch marks. Olive oil or vitamin E oil are good options; so are lavender oil and aloe vera. Their regular use can minimize the appearance of the stretch marks.

Nutrition and Exercise

If you're overweight, lose the flab! Losing body fat and increasing muscle tone through diet and exercise will firm up areas blighted by stretch marks and reduce their visibility. Eat foods high in "beauty" nutrients such as vitamins A and C (concentrated in fruits and vegetables), vitamin D (found in low-fat milk and low-fat cheese), and zinc (found in meat, fish, nuts, and beans)—all nutrients that promote healthy skin.

Hydration

Drink at least eight glasses of water a day to keep your skin pliable and resistant to stretch marks. Plus, you'll definitely be the best-looking gal in the restroom. Limit coffee, tea, and cola consumption because they dehydrate your body.

My Favorite Home Remedy

Peanut butter is great with jelly on a sandwich, and it can double as shaving gel to shave your legs (use smooth peanut butter, please, not chunky), and clean leather. And did you know that peanut butter is a great remedy for removing stretch marks? Make a concoction of 2 tablespoons of peanut butter and 1 tablespoon of vegetable shortening. Apply the mixture to your stretch marks and leave it there for 15 minutes before washing it off. Do this three times a week, and you'll notice your stretch marks get much less visible.

Like most things cosmetic, stretch marks require attack from multiple fronts. Try the following program for seven days.

 # Day 1

MORNING ROUTINE

Apply a topical cream containing Centella asiatica (such as Mederma) in a circular motion on all areas of your body where you have stretch marks.

Take 500 milligrams of vitamin C with your breakfast. Take a multivitamin/multimineral tablet containing zinc. Zinc is effective against stretch marks.

NOON

Take 500 milligrams of vitamin C with your lunch.

AFTERNOON/EARLY EVENING

Do yoga today. It's beneficial for toning muscles and making your skin more elastic, which helps stretch marks fade gradually.

DINNER

Take 500 milligrams of vitamin C with your dinner.

EVENING ROUTINE

Again, apply a topical cream containing Centella asiatica (such as Mederma) in a circular motion on all areas of your body where you have stretch marks.

Day 2

MORNING ROUTINE

Apply a topical cream containing Centella asiatica (such as Mederma) over your stretch marks.

Take 500 milligrams of vitamin C with your breakfast, along with a multivitamin/multimineral tablet.

NOON

Take 500 milligrams of vitamin C with your lunch.

DINNER

Take 500 milligrams of vitamin C with your dinner.

EVENING ROUTINE

Apply my peanut butter treatment as recommended.

Day 3

MORNING ROUTINE

Apply a topical cream containing Centella asiatica (such as Mederma) over your stretch marks.

Take 500 milligrams of vitamin C with your breakfast, along with a multivitamin/multimineral tablet.

NOON

Take 500 milligrams of vitamin C with your lunch.

DINNER

Take 500 milligrams of vitamin C with your dinner.

EVENING ROUTINE

Apply a topical cream containing Centella asiatica (such as Mederma) over your stretch marks.

Day 4

MORNING ROUTINE

Apply a topical cream containing Centella asiatica (such as Mederma) over your stretch marks.

Take 500 milligrams of vitamin C with your breakfast. Take a multivitamin/multimineral tablet containing zinc. Zinc is effective against stretch marks.

NOON

Take 500 milligrams of vitamin C with your lunch.

AFTERNOON/EARLY EVENING

Attend a Pilates or a yoga–Pilates fusion class. Both can work miracles on stretch marks.

Try minimizing the appearance of your stretch marks with an all-over artificial tan. Just make sure it's waterproof.

DINNER

Take 500 milligrams of vitamin C with your dinner.

EVENING ROUTINE

Apply my peanut butter treatment as recommended.

 Day 5

MORNING ROUTINE

Apply a topical cream containing Centella asiatica (such as Mederma) over your stretch marks. If you're not getting results from this, use a moisturizing oil like vitamin E oil on the affected areas regularly. This will reduce the appearance of stretch marks. Apply it after a shower so that gets absorbed into the skin quickly. Or try cocoa butter. It helps diminish the appearance of these marks, especially following pregnancy. Pure cocoa butter is most effective and can be applied directly to the stretch mark several times a day.

Take 500 milligrams of vitamin C with your breakfast, plus a multivitamin/multimineral tablet containing zinc.

NOON
Take 500 milligrams of vitamin C with your lunch.

AFTERNOON/EARLY EVENING
Do yoga or Pilates today.

DINNER
Take 500 milligrams of vitamin C with your dinner.

EVENING ROUTINE
Apply a topical cream containing Centella asiatica (such as Mederma) over your stretch marks. Or apply pure cocoa butter.

Day 6

MORNING ROUTINE
Apply a topical cream containing Centella asiatica (such as Mederma) over your stretch marks. Alternatively, apply vitamin E oil or pure cocoa butter after you shower.

Take 500 milligrams of vitamin C with your breakfast, plus a multivitamin/multimineral tablet containing zinc.

NOON
Take 500 milligrams of vitamin C with your lunch.

AFTERNOON/EARLY EVENING
Do Pilates or yoga today.

DINNER
Take 500 milligrams of vitamin C with your dinner.

EVENING ROUTINE
Apply my peanut butter treatment as recommended.

Day 7

MORNING ROUTINE

Apply a topical cream containing Centella asiatica (such as Mederma) over your stretch marks. Alternatively, apply vitamin E oil or pure cocoa butter after you shower.

Take 500 milligrams of vitamin C with your breakfast. Take a multi-vitamin/multimineral tablet containing zinc. Zinc is effective against stretch marks.

NOON

Take 500 milligrams of vitamin C with your lunch.

AFTERNOON/EARLY EVENING

Do Pilates or yoga today.

DINNER

Take 500 milligrams of vitamin C with your dinner.

EVENING ROUTINE

Apply a topical cream containing Centella asiatica (such as Mederma) over your stretch marks. Or apply pure cocoa butter.

Instead of using a full-on fake tan, go for a more natural look by using a moisturizer with a hint of added tanner.

Stretch marks can happen to anyone. Minimizing them takes a regular, focused routine. Continue these measures, and those unsexy marks will eventually fade into oblivion.

fewer unsightly veins in 7

Are your legs beginning to resemble a series of spider webs? If so, understand that as a woman, you have thinner skin than men have, which means you're destined to face the problem of those reddish, bluish, or purple veins on your legs; *telanglectasia*, commonly referred to as "spider veins." They pop up when your body's estrogen levels are elevated: during pregnancy, when taking oral contraceptives or estrogen replacement therapy, and even during menstruation. They're also common in people who stand regularly in their jobs, such as nurses, cashiers, or hair stylists. Standing increases the venous pressure in the legs and can cause the veins to stretch. Even if you sit a great deal, you can also develop spider veins, because sitting slows circulation. Heredity also plays a role; if your mother had them, you will probably get them, too.

In my practice, I go after spider veins with sclerotherapy (injections). This involves the injection of a solution such as hypertonic saline, into each vein, causing it to collapse, become scar tissue, and disappear. Then, my favorite therapy came along at last: intense light therapy (like a laser). It doesn't irritate the surrounding tissues. Success rates of treatment are very high, though not 100 percent, but a trip to your doctor can help you decide your options.

Now, if you're not interested in taking a treatment route, you may be able to minimize the appearance of spider veins, and even stop them from worsening, with several natural treatments I've incorporated into my seven-day program.

One of these treatments involves supplementation. There are several dietary supplements on the market, for example, made of either grape seed extract or horse chestnut extract, which claim to improve the appearance of leg veins by increasing circulation. These products, with names like Vein Health or Venastat, are taken in pill form and are usually available at health food, grocery, or drug stores for less than $15. Be sure to check with your doctor before trying any of these supplements. I advise women who are pregnant, are breast feeding, or have liver, heart, or circulation problems to stay away from these products, however.

As for nutrition, your first nutritional line of defense should be vitamin C. It's critical to the body's production of collagen, which is the fibrous protein that builds and repairs blood vessels and other tissues. Fresh, whole sources of the vitamin are the best. Citrus fruits with thick skins like oranges and grapefruits are packed with vitamin C. Choose two to three servings of these foods each day.

If you'd rather take a vitamin C supplement as extra insurance, opt for one that comes combined with bioflavonoids, plant components that improve the permeability, and integrity of capillary walls. Good food sources of bioflavonoids are apricots, green peppers, broccoli, tomatoes, tea, and the white skin and membranes of citrus fruit. Have three to four servings of these foods daily. The recommended daily intake of vitamin C with bioflavonoids is 500 to 3,000 milligrams daily.

Eating foods high in vitamin K, such as kelp, alfalfa, green leafy vegetables, meat, and cheese, has been reported to be beneficial. Have one serving of vitamin K food a day.

Now here's my seven-day routine.

Day 1

MORNING ROUTINE

Starting today, twice a day (in the morning and at bedtime) apply a vitamin K cream. That's the best type to use, in my opinion, because it has been used since the 1930s by cosmetic surgeons to help heal bruises after surgical procedures. If it works on bruises, it should also work on spider veins since the causes are so similar. After all, a bruise is simply damage to blood vessels that causes pooling of blood and discoloration to the skin. The vitamin K is carried from the skin into capillaries where it strengthens and repairs the damaged blood vessels. Two products to consider are Dermal-K and Veinish. They appear to work by penetrating the skin to reduce the appearance of the veins.

Take one dose of Vein Health or Venastat after breakfast with a full glass of water.

EVENING ROUTINE

Treat spider veins with the following home remedy: Wrap the areas affected by spider veins with soft cloths soaked in apple cider vinegar. Leave the wrap on for 30 minutes. Do this at least once a day; it may improve the appearance of spider veins after about eight weeks.

Apply vitamin K cream to the affected area.

TODAY'S WORKOUT

As I've said again and again, exercise increases circulation—and that's just what your body needs to stop the development of more spider veins. Each day, do my recommended exercise to keep blood flowing healthfully.

Calf raises: You need a stable, firm raised area, like the first step on your stairs at home. Stand on the step with both feet so that your heels extend over the edge of the step. Hold on to a wall or rail for balance. Raise yourself up on your toes, and lower your heels down below the step. Repeat 30 to 50 times. You should feel the stretch at the back of your calf muscles. Do the exercise at least once a day and ideally twice.

Elevate your legs above the level of your heart for 10 to 15 minutes three or four times per day.

 ## Day 2

MORNING ROUTINE

Apply vitamin K cream to the affected area.

Take one dose of Vein Health or Venastat after breakfast with a full glass of water.

EVENING ROUTINE

Apply vitamin K cream to the affected area.

TODAY'S WORKOUT

Tiptoe walking: While working around the house, walk on tiptoes. This stretches and activates muscles in the calf area. Okay, so you feel a little stupid, but who cares?

Elevate your legs above the level of your heart for 10 to 15 minutes three or four times per day.

 ## Day 3

MORNING ROUTINE

Apply vitamin K cream to the affected area.

Take one dose of Vein Health or Venastat after breakfast with a full glass of water.

EVENING ROUTINE

Wrap the spider veins with soft cloths soaked in apple cider vinegar for 30 minutes.

Apply vitamin K cream to the affected area.

TODAY'S WORKOUT
Heel walking: Instead of walking around on tiptoes, raise your toes off the ground and walk on your heels. This might feel even more stupid, but it's a great simple exercise for your calves.

ADDITIONAL ACTIONS

Elevate your legs above the level of your heart for 10 to 15 minutes three or four times per day.

 Day 4

MORNING ROUTINE
Apply vitamin K cream to the affected area.

Take one dose of Vein Health or Venastat after breakfast with a full glass of water.

EVENING ROUTINE
Apply vitamin K cream to the affected area.

TODAY'S WORKOUT
Foot rocking: Try this exercise if you're sitting for long periods of time (like at your desk or in an airplane). Raise your toes so that your heel is the only point of contact with the floor. Then place the foot back down elevate the heel so your toes are in contact with the floor. Perform this in a single rocking movement with both feet at once.

ADDITIONAL ACTIONS

Elevate your legs above the level of your heart for 10 to 15 minutes three or four times per day.

Day 5

MORNING ROUTINE

Apply vitamin K cream to the affected area.

Take one dose of Vein Health or Venastat after breakfast with a full glass of water.

EVENING ROUTINE

Wrap the area affected by spider veins in soft cloths soaked in apple cider vinegar. Leave the wrap on for thirty minutes.

Apply vitamin K cream to the affected area.

TODAY'S WORKOUT

Take a brisk 45 to 60 minute walk.

ADDITIONAL ACTIONS

Elevate your legs above the level of your heart for 10 to 15 minutes three or four times per day.

 Day 6

MORNING ROUTINE

Apply vitamin K cream to the affected area.

Take one dose of Vein Health or Venastat after breakfast with a full glass of water.

EVENING ROUTINE

Apply vitamin K cream to the affected area.

TODAY'S WORKOUT

Walking Dumbbell Lunges (see page 73).

ADDITIONAL ACTIONS

Elevate your legs above the level of your heart for 10 to 15 minutes three or four times per day.

Day 7

MORNING ROUTINE

Apply vitamin K cream to the affected area.

Take one dose of Vein Health or Venastat after breakfast with a full glass of water.

EVENING ROUTINE

Wrap the area affected by spider veins in soft cloths soaked in apple cider vinegar. Leave the wrap on for thirty minutes.

Apply vitamin K cream to the affected areas.

ADDITIONAL ACTIONS

Elevate your legs above the level of your heart for 10 to 15 minutes three or four times per day.

Fair warning: You must be prepared to commit to this routine to see any improvement. So, stick with this plan—even beyond the first seven days.

➡ 7 WAYS TO MINIMIZE SPIDER VEINS

1. **Wear sunscreen.** Too much sun exposure can cause spider veins. That's because harmful ultraviolet light breaks down collagen, which composes the walls of spider veins, and can cause thinning and spreading of the veins.

2. **Exercise regularly to improve your leg strength, circulation, and vein strength.** Focus on exercises that work your legs, such as walking or running.

3. **Lose weight.** Excess weight puts too much pressure on your legs.

4. **Add strength-training exercises to your workout to help keep legs toned, strong, and agile.** Strong leg muscles actually massage the veins in your legs—an action that prevents spider veins, as well as varicose veins.

5. **Don't stand for prolonged periods.** If you have to stand for long periods of time, shift your weight from one leg to the other every few minutes.

6. **Have no fear of support hose.** Today's versions are chic and stylish. Many experts believe that keeping the legs compressed helps prevent spider veins.

7. **Ditch those killer heels.** You may have a love affair with your spiked heels, but they do nothing for your leg vein health. High heels put extra strain on your veins, so wear them only occasionally.

CHAPTER 10
sexier hair in 7

When asked what type of tresses turns them on, most men will tell you Rapunzel-type hair that falls past your shoulders and halfway down your back. Okay, even if you don't have that kind of va-va-voom hair, you can still satisfy his—and your—lust for long, sexy locks. Let's talk about how.

You "hair what you eat," honey. A diet rich in vegetables, lean protein, complex carbohydrates, and monounsaturated fats—such as olive oil and avocados—is what gives your body the nutrients it needs to grow healthy hair.

If you were sitting in my office right now, I'd be able to tell if you're not eating that kind of diet. Your hair might be lifeless, dull, and dry—all signs of nutritional deficiencies—which is why eating well-rounded meals is the best strategy for getting healthier hair. But honestly, for a lot of women, a perfectly balanced diet 24/7 is unrealistic. So, what's the nutritional solution? I recommend certain supplements to fill in the gaps. If you're eating a less-than-stellar diet, supplements can keep your hair growing at its maximum speed of half an inch per month.

My recommended supplement protocol includes the following:

- **Time-release multivitamins containing 100 percent of the daily requirements of vitamins A, B, C, and E.** All of these vitamins contribute to healthy hair in various ways. Vitamin A enhances the health of the sebaceous glands in the scalp. B vitamins help circulation, protect the health of hair follicles and regulate growth processes (including those of hair) in the body. Vitamin C protects hair from undue breakage, and vitamin E enhances scalp circulation and hair quality.

- **Biotin (at least 300 micrograms a day).** Dubbed the hair vitamin, biotin helps produce healthy hair and may even help prevent balding. It also helps your body utilize protein and is involved in the production of keratin, the protein in hair and nails.

- **L-cysteine (at least 500 milligrams a day).** This amino acid is involved in the formation of skin and hair.

- **Gamma linolenic acid (GLA) (at least 240 milligrams a day in the form of evening primrose oil or black currant oil).** This friendly fat can be helpful in hair loss caused by a deficiency in essential fatty acids.

- **Biosil (contains a silicon and choline, a B vitamin).** This product has been found to benefit hair, skin, and nails, according to a study published in the *Archives of Dermatological Research*. In a group of 50 women between the ages of 40 and 65, half took 10 milligrams of BioSil, while the rest took a placebo. After 20 weeks, the supplement-takers had smoother, more elastic skin, a 30 percent reduction in wrinkle depth, and less brittle hair and nails, compared to those taking the placebo.

- **Then there's exercise, something I keep harping on in practically every chapter, but it does produce miracles.** Okay, I know what you're thinking: What on earth does exercise have to do with healthy hair? Answer: one helluva lot! Exercising improves your body's circulation: A pounding heart pumps more blood to your hair follicles, which in turn improves hair. So, work out for healthier hair.

☐ **You can also stimulate circulation with a vigorous daily scalp massage.** With your fingertips, massage your scalp using small circular motions for about three minutes. Even better, try my Scalp-Stimulating Tonic.

✚ DR. ORDON'S SCALP-STIMULATING TONIC

Rosemary essential oil has been used for centuries to encourage hair growth. To make my Scalp-Stimulating Tonic, mix five drops of rosemary oil with one capsule-full of vitamin E and 1 teaspoon of grapeseed oil. Massage into your scalp. Cover your head with a plastic shower cap. Try to leave it on for 20 to 30 minutes for greatest penetration; then wash off with a mild shampoo.

Now it's time for my seven-day program for healthier hair.

 # Day 1

MORNING ROUTINE

My recommended breakfast every day is 1 tablespoon of wheat germ, 1 tablespoon of brewer's yeast (a natural source of hair-healthy B vitamins), 1 tablespoon lecithin, 1 tablespoon agave nectar, and 1 cup of nonfat Greek yogurt. Combine all ingredients in the yogurt, and eat it for breakfast this week. In seven days, you will see results —a hair full of strength and growing faster.

Take your supplements with breakfast.

MORNING OR EVENING

Massage your scalp using my tonic. Then wash your hair with shampoo; add a teaspoon of baking soda to the amount of shampoo you use on your hair. It will help remove residue and add shine to your hair.

But don't overwash this week. Shampooing every day is drying to your hair and scalp. Instead, aim for two to three times a week. On off days, rinse with water and condition only your ends.

After shampooing, take a can of warm flat beer and pour it through your hair. The protein from the malt and hops help repair damaged hair, plus adds body and shine.

Get in at least 45 minutes of some circulation-boosting cardio activity: walking, jogging, cardio machine training, cycling, swimming, or aerobic dance.

 ## Day 2

MORNING ROUTINE
Take your supplements with my recommended breakfast.

MORNING OR EVENING ROUTINE
Apply an "onion rub." Onions are loaded with sulfur, a hair-healing mineral. Rub half an onion into your scalp to help stimulate hair growth. Rinse your hair well with warm water.

As a snack, enjoy a glass (8 ounces) of organic carrot juice. Carrots also carry other vitamins such as B, C, D, E, and K, and minerals like calcium, phosphorous, potassium, sodium, and traces of protein. Carrot juice helps promote healthier hair.

 ## Day 3

MORNING ROUTINE
Take your supplements with my recommended breakfast.

MORNING OR EVENING ROUTINE
Massage your scalp using my tonic. Then wash your hair with shampoo; add a teaspoon of baking soda. Rinse with one can of warm, flat beer.

Get in at least 45 minutes of some circulation-boosting cardio activity: walking, jogging, cardio machine training, cycling, swimming, or aerobic dance.

Day 4

MORNING ROUTINE

Take your supplements with my recommended breakfast.

Deep-condition your hair, using my Deep Conditioning Treatment.

✚ DR. ORDON'S DEEP CONDITIONING TREATMENT

Mix together:

- ½ cup mayonnaise
- 1 tablespoon coconut oil
- 1 teaspoon coconut extract

Apply conditioner and cover your scalp with plastic wrap (such as Saran Wrap). Leave on for 20 to 30 minutes; then rinse your hair thoroughly.

MORNING OR EVENING ROUTINE

As a snack, enjoy a glass (8 ounces) of organic carrot juice.

Day 5

MORNING ROUTINE

Take your supplements with my recommended breakfast.

MORNING OR EVENING ROUTINE

Rub one half of an onion into your scalp to help stimulate hair growth.

Then wash your hair with shampoo; add a teaspoon of baking soda. Rinse with one can of warm, flat beer.

Get in at least 45 minutes of some circulation-boosting cardio activity: walking, jogging, cardio machine training, cycling, swimming, or aerobic dance.

Day 6

MORNING ROUTINE
Take your supplements with my recommended breakfast.

MORNING OR EVENING ROUTINE
Massage your scalp using my tonic.

As a snack, enjoy a glass (8 ounces) of organic carrot juice.

Day 7

MORNING ROUTINE
Take your supplements with my recommended breakfast.

MORNING OR EVENING ROUTINE
Shampoo your hair (add baking soda); then rinse with beer. Next, deep-condition your hair, using my Deep Conditioning Treatment.

Get in at least 45 minutes of some circulation-boosting cardio activity: walking, jogging, cardio machine training, cycling, swimming, or aerobic dance.

➡ SPECIAL CASE: IF YOU'RE LOSING YOUR HAIR

Your hair is one of your most defining characteristics. So, when it's thinning or coming out in clumps, it can be devastating. Please see your dermatologist at the first noticeable signs of hair loss. They will be able to diagnose the problem, which may fall into one of three categories:

- **Female-pattern hair loss.** The most common form of hair loss in women is female-pattern hair loss, a hereditary condition characterized by visible thinning over the crown. Rest assured, it can be successfully treated. Minoxidil 2% is the only topical medication approved by the U.S. Food and Drug Administration (FDA) for this type of hair loss. It is available over the counter. Minoxidil does not grow new hair; rather, it works by prolonging the growth phase of hair, allowing more time for hair to grow out to its full density. You must apply minoxidil every day.

Other treatments include finasteride (which is FDA-approved for male-pattern hair loss) for women of nonchildbearing age only, as well as the drugs spironolactone and flutamide, which work by blocking the male hormone testosterone at the cellular level of the hair follicle. These oral medications also may be an option if you don't want to spend time applying minoxidil every day.

□ **Telogen effluvium.** This is the second most common form of hair loss, usually triggered by severe physical or emotional stress. For example, surgery, childbirth, dramatic weight loss (including gastric bypass surgery), the death of a loved one, iron deficiency, and chronic thyroid diseases can trigger telogen effluvium. Once the stressor is removed, hair growth gradually returns to normal, but it can take anywhere from three to nine months.

□ **Alopecia areata.** It starts with a tiny bald spot on your head, no bigger than the tip of a felt marker. Within months, it spreads to the size of a penny and then a quarter. Before long, you can lose all your hair. You're suffering from alopecia areata, an autoimmune form of hair loss that can affect men and women. It occurs when your body's own white blood cells attack the hair follicles and put them to sleep. Although there are no FDA-approved treatments for alopecia areata, your dermatologist may prescribe combination therapies such as injectable steroids, topical steroids, or minoxidil 5% to try to regrow hair in patches of bald spots.

PART 3
younger in 7

To quote humorist and author Mark Twain, "Age is an issue of mind over matter. If you don't mind, it doesn't matter."

In reality, though, getting older and seeing wrinkles develop where smooth, youthful skin once was can be hard to deal with. If you've wanted to turn back the clock but without having a cosmetic procedure, you've come to the right part of this book. In truth, a wide range of natural treatments are available that offer immediate results with no downtime and are very affordable. Even though I'm a plastic surgeon, I feel that it's more beneficial to choose nonsurgical procedures because you can keep a natural look versus a dramatic change. And each wrinkle or fine line has a story—you don't want to remove *all* of them! It's not realistic to be wrinkle-free. You want to look great for your age. Try the following programs to look younger in seven days. And the next time you go to your high-school reunion, wear a plastic name tag with a photo on it—one that's a "before" photo (before you tried the programs in this part)—so all your old classmates will recognize you when they see the "new improved you" at the event. Just say, "Hi, I'm Debbie. I used to look like this."

One piece of advice on aging: Don't ever worry about turning another year older. Birthdays are good for you. People who have the most birthdays live the longest.

fewer wrinkles in 7

Every time you laugh, smile, frown, cry, pucker your lips, raise your eyebrows, or squint your eyes, the muscles of your face contract, temporarily folding your skin into creases. In your youth, when your skin is firm, supple, and elastic, these lines of expression vanish immediately as your muscles relax and your skin springs back to smoothness.

But with age, years of sun exposure, declining hormones, bad habits like smoking, and other skin ravagers, your skin loses its youthful bounce. No longer can it retract with its earlier pliability. It begins the process of acquiring, over time, permanent lines—*wrinkles*—on those areas of your face most subject to muscular contractions. "Crow's-feet" fan out from the corner of your eyes, marionette lines run parallel to your nose and mouth, and frown lines get etched into your forehead and between your brows.

Call them what you will, wrinkles aren't life-threatening, fortunately, but I know you'd rather not have them staring back at you in the mirror. I've had plenty of women come into my office who have given themselves their own temporary "face-lift" by using tape, clips, or headbands to actually pull the skin of their face taut. They actually walk around this way, that is, until they come into my office. Then they undo what they have done and say, "See what happens when I take the tape way." This may sound a bit extreme, but if you've celebrated a few decades' worth of birthdays and have noticed fine lines and wrinkles, you're certainly not alone. (After all, anti-aging skincare is an $832 million market.)

Though signs of aging can appear in your 20s, you generally start seeing them in your early to mid-30s. Wrinkles, lines, and sagging are all part of the natural aging process, and whether you get them or how severe depends on several things. First, there's no question that what you inherited from your mom and dad plays a role in how your skin ages. But beyond that, outside factors have an impact. The biggest is sun damage. In fact, experts believe that only 20 percent of aging is the result of genetics and that the remaining 80 percent is caused by a lifetime of sun exposure, according to the American Academy of Dermatology. That's because UV light has a direct, negative effect on your skin at the cellular level by causing the formation of free radicals, which damage your epidermis, the outermost layer of the skin, the dermis, the layer beneath this, and skin's fibroblasts, the cells that produce collagen and elastin. These are two of the key components of youthful-looking skin. In young skin, fibroblasts are plentiful and work well, so the collagen is firm and there's lots of it. However, this changes with the natural aging process, so by the time you hit your 80s, you typically have four times more damaged collagen than a 20-year-old.

Repetitive movements also have an impact on the lines that criss-cross your complexion, because the way you use your muscles affects where and how you form wrinkles. If you're repetitively pursing your lips, frowning, squinting, or scowling, it's going to show up on your face.

Another aspect of aging is that we lose some of our subcutaneous facial fat, which keeps skin plump. The result is a more sunken look, and because some of the skin's supportive structure is gone, sagging occurs. But enough of the bad news. There are plenty of lifestyle changes that can actually improve the appearance of your lines and wrinkles and prevent future ones.

More than ever before, there are more ways to erase wrinkles, from injectable fillers to chemical peels to laser resurfacing. I use Botox, Dysport, and Xeomin every day on frown lines and crow's-feet, for example. Botox is injected into skin to paralyze the muscles that control repetitive movements and create wrinkles. It's typically used on the forehead, between the brows and around the eyes. Botox injections last about three to four months. Or I might add volume back into your face using synthetic fillers or your own body fat. How long these fillers last depends on which one is used. Some last a matter of months to a year while others are permanent.

I also use lasers and radiofrequency devices to resurface the skin. Each device works a bit differently, but the general idea is that they remove the top layer of skin and heat it so that as it heals, it gets tighter and stimulates the production of new collagen.

But what if you want to get rid of wrinkles quickly and without these semi-invasive and often costly procedures?

There are hundreds of ways to achieve newer, more refreshed, and revitalized skin, with diminished wrinkling, and most plastic surgeons now recommend a mix of traditional procedures and natural treatments. In my practice, I've seen women look 10 to 15 years younger in just seven days by following a skincare regime of natural remedies, a supplemented diet, and healthier lifestyle.

So, the question is, what should you be doing, starting today, to turn back the hands of time, or at least slow them down?

Answer: It depends largely on the current condition of your complexion and its degree of wrinkling. No two women have exactly the same skin or skin conditions. But there are products, treatments, and procedures designed for practically every situation. Here, I'll be focusing on wrinkles, and there are several basic actions you can take, regardless of age or skin condition, to prevent wrinkles, slow their formation, and achieve smoother skin in general. Let's take a look.

Fortify Yourself Nutritionally

Now for some "duh" advice: What your skin needs most of all is a healthy lifestyle. Translation: healthy diet. That's easier said than done, so what I recommend is that you simply eat my Wrinkle Reducing Fruit Salad daily for breakfast. It's loaded with antioxidants, which combat "free radicals." It sounds like a call to arms against terrorists, doesn't it? But those nasty free radicals actually kill cells and age you. Combat them by taking antioxidants, which you can get in this salad and all fruits and veggies.

Antioxidants protect skin from sun damage and enhance circulation to give skin the nutrients it needs.

This fruit salad is full of antioxidants. One is vitamin C, which helps increase the skin's production of collagen, repair cellular damage, and keep blood vessels healthy. Blueberries and pomegranates also contain high levels of anthocyanins, a type of antioxidant that can help fight the signs of aging. The walnuts contain omega-3 essential fatty acids that are important for strengthening the outermost layer of the skin and reducing dryness so your complexion glows and lines are less noticeable.

✚ DR. ORDON'S WRINKLE-REDUCING FRUIT SALAD

INGREDIENTS:

- ½ cup fresh blueberries
- ½ cup fresh strawberries
- 1 kiwi, peeled and chopped
- ½ cup pomegranate seeds
- ½ cup organic orange juice
- 1 handful of chopped walnuts

INSTRUCTIONS:
Combine the first four ingredients in small bowl. Pour the orange juice over the mixture and sprinkle with the walnuts.

At lunch or dinner, include some orange veggies in your diet to capitalize on their antioxidant power. Sweet potatoes, carrots, and other orange veggies contain beta-carotene, a compound that your body can actually convert into vitamin A, which is retinol. This is the same ingredient in many topical wrinkle products. Beta carotene also enhances the skin's ability to slough off dead skin cells, something that decreases as we age. Agave is a natural sweetener, and matcha green tea powder offers all the antioxidant benefits of green tea but in high enough concentrations to actually make a difference.

As for other fruits and vegetables, the more colorful your meals, the more packed it is with anti-wrinkle vitamins and nutrients. But careful on the preparation: Cook the hell out of them, and you lose some vital nutrients. What do I recommend? Steam your veggies to capitalize on their anti-wrinkle power.

My "Anti-wrinkle Mash" is a side dish that delivers an antioxidant punch. My patients love it.

✚ DR. ORDON'S ANTI-WRINKLE MASH

INGREDIENTS:

- ☐ 1 skinless baked sweet potato
- ☐ 1 cup of carrots, cooked
- ☐ 1 tablespoon agave nectar
- ☐ 1 tablespoon matcha green tea powder

INSTRUCTIONS:

Combine the sweet potato and carrots. Mash well. Add the agave and matcha powder and mix well. Serve hot.

Supplement Against Wrinkles

As extra insurance, I advise my patients to take supplements in order to circumvent skin damage. Based on available evidence on anti-wrinkle nutrients, I recommend the following supplement protocol:

☐ **A once-a-day vitamin-mineral tablet containing antioxidant nutrients.** Damaged skin cells can lead to accelerated aging in the form of wrinkles, dry skin, dark circles under eyes, dull skin, and more. Ensure against the damage by taking a multiple every day.

- ☐ **200 international units of vitamin E.** This antioxidant decelerates aging in two important ways. First, it interferes with the production of an enzyme called *collagenase*, which breaks down collagen, causing your skin to sag and wrinkle. Second, it protects against sun damage. Sun exposure can deplete vitamin E from the skin. With vitamin E in short supply, your skin is more vulnerable to sun damage (which is why vitamin E is found in skin-care products from moisturizers to body washes). Taking a vitamin E supplements daily can have profound effects on your skin's texture and can decrease wrinkles and sun damage.

- ☐ **500 milligrams of vitamin C.** As you get older, your body slows down its production of collagen and elastin, which are two proteins that keep your skin strong, flexible, and resilient. Evidence suggests that supplemental vitamin C may stimulate the production of collagen and minimize fine lines and wrinkles.

- ☐ **50 to 100 milligrams of alpha lipoic acid (ALA).** This antioxidant boosts the effects of other antioxidants. But ALA has another advantage: It can help keep your skin looking young, whether taken orally or applied topically to the skin.

- ☐ **Up to 50 micrograms of selenium.** This antioxidant mineral encourages tissue elasticity and powerfully protects against sun damage.

- ☐ **12 milligrams of zinc.** This trace mineral helps maintain collagen and elastin, helping to prevent sagging and wrinkles. It also links together amino acids that are needed for the formation of collagen.

- ☐ **500 milligrams of either Evening Primrose Oil or Borage Oil.** Your skin is guarded by a barrier called the *stratum corneum* that keeps it water tight. Assaults to the stratum corneum can result in water loss, which dehydrates the skin and gives it a dry, wrinkly appearance. Taking evening primrose oil or borage oil improves dry, sensitive skin by replenishing essential components of the stratum corneum.

Water Your Skin

Water is your skin's best friend. It keeps your skin supple and resilient. Each day drink at least three glasses of iced or hot green tea. Along with this have at least six glasses of regular water with lemon. You're plumping skin from within.

Lifestyle Fixes

How you live affects how well—or how poorly—your skin ages. Here are some suggestions for keeping wrinkles at bay:

- **Change the way you sleep.** When you sleep on your side, the skin on that side of your face bunches up. Over time, this can lead to permanent lines on your cheeks and around the eyes. For the next seven days, sleep on your back; just make sure to slip a small pillow under your knees to put your body in an ergonomically correct position taking pressure off your back. Also, get yourself a satin pillowcase. This way, if you do roll over to your side, the satin fabric's slippery surface bunches the skin up less than cotton.

- **Put out your cigarettes.** Seriously, sweetie, don't smoke. Lung cancer and emphysema aside, it causes premature wrinkles and yellow teeth, making you look like those old timers who play the slots in casinos.

    Quitting smoking may be easier said than done, but the reasons why you should do so are endless. Naturally, there are many health risks that increase when you smoke. But when it comes to your complexion, smoking affects the basic physiology of your skin cells. This is why a smoker's skin ages faster and doesn't look as healthy as a nonsmoker's.

    First, smoking damages the fine, sensitive blood vessels in the skin. This reduces the subdermal blood supply and the circulation to the skin, which is why a smoker's complexion can look dull and sallow. This damaged blood supply also means a smoker's skin won't heal as well as a nonsmoker's from anything, be it a pimple or a face-lift.

(This is why it's so risky for us plastic surgeons to do a face-lift on a smoker.)

Second, the nicotine and tars in cigarettes promote disease-causing, cell- and collagen-damaging free radicals. Lastly, the repetitive motion of pursing your lips to puff on a cigarette can cause wrinkles.

If you quit, you can do it cold turkey or try cutting down gradually to one smoke a day, as one of my patients did. At that point, kicking the habit altogether won't actually be that hard. Being a one-cigarette-a-day smoker does have its dilemmas, however. For example, will you be lying when you fill out an insurance application and, to get a reduced rate, claim you're a non-smoker? Enough said, don't continue to ignore the surgeon general's warning.

□ **Control some of your repetitive movements.** Laughing and smiling are repetitive movements you should never try to stop. But you can avoid others that etch wrinkles into your face. Don't sip all your beverages through a straw. When done on a regular basis, this habit can cause or worsen lip lines. And always, always wear sunglasses outside to prevent squinting and damage to thin eye area skin.

Exfoliate

Exfoliation—the process of sloughing off dead skin cells—helps loosen dead skin cells and makes your skin look smoother. There are two types of exfoliation: natural and chemical. Chemical exfoliants include hydroxyl acids, tretinoin (Renova or Retin-A), and chemical peels.

Hydroxy acids are natural-based acids found in many skin-care products includes glycolic, lactic, citric, and tartaric acids. Glycolic acid was the original AHA and works well for reducing fine lines, age spots, and acne scars. Peels with higher concentrations of AHAs are usually administered by an esthetician or dermatologist, but lower concentrations—between 5 percent and 10 percent—are available in creams or lotions. (I don't recommend these products, though, if you're older than 50 because they dry out the skin and this can actually lead to wrinkles.)

Vitamin A and its derivatives are powerful and proven anti-aging antioxidants. Retinol is a topical ingredient that stimulates collagen production and plumps out your skin, reducing fine lines and wrinkles. It also improves skin tone and color and reduces mottled patches (hyperpigmentation) on the skin. Many dermatologists prescribe retinol's stronger counterparts, Retin A or Renova. Over-the-counter products containing retinols may be weaker but are still effective in improving skin appearance.

Natural exfoliants include washcloths, loofahs, or cleansing grains or scrubs; they work by rubbing and stimulating the skin and are good for most skin types. My seven-day plan focuses on a natural exfoliant, the Sugar Facial Scrub, that you can whip up in your kitchen.

✚ DR. ORDON'S SUGAR FACIAL SCRUB RECIPE

INGREDIENTS:

- ▫ 3 tablespoons of fresh cream
- ▫ 1 cup of white sugar
- ▫ ½ cup of brown sugar
- ▫ ½ cup of ground almonds
- ▫ 2 tablespoons olive oil

INSTRUCTIONS:

Mix all ingredients well. Apply to dry face, in a circular motion. Wash your face off with warm water, followed by cold water. Pat your face dry. Place in a jar and store in your refrigerator for future use.

You can also exfoliate and minimize your wrinkles with seaweed. Recently, seaweed has become a popular ingredient in many skincare products, and it's easy to see why. Seaweed is rich in so many of the vitamins and minerals that skin needs to look healthy. These include potassium, calcium, magnesium, phosphorus, iron, zinc, and manganese and nutrients like folic acid and niacin. Seaweed also helps exfoliate dead skin cells, oils, and dirt and hydrates so skin looks more radiant and plumper and so fine lines look less noticeable. Apply this seaweed facial mask two to three times per week.

➕ DR. ORDON'S SEAWEED MASK

INGREDIENTS:

- ½ cup of sea veg flakes (also called *agar*, available at most health food stores or the ethnic aisle of many supermarkets)
- 1 to 2 tablespoons of water

DIRECTIONS:
Combine the water with the sea veg flakes. Mix until both are well combined. Add more water if mixture is too thick. Spread this onto damp facial skin for 10 to 15 minutes. Rinse thoroughly. Use this mask two to three times a week.

Moisturize

Moisturizers are not anti-wrinkle products *per se*, but I feel they are underrated as wrinkle fighters, for three reasons. First, they treat dry skin. When skin dries out, it looks as wrinkly as a prune. Moisturizers encourage the skin to hold and retain moisture, making your complexion look smooth and refreshed.

Second, moisturizers act as temporary fillers. The solid material found in these products fills in the tiny crevices of wrinkles, making your skin look smoother. Of course, this is only a temporary effect, lasting six to eight hours, but it improves the appearance of wrinkles nonetheless.

Third, some moisturizers contain cosmetically inactive ingredients that reflect light away from your face, making wrinkles far less noticeable.

There are thousands and thousands of moisturizers on the market; you really have to experiment to find one that is compatible with your skin. On my seven-day program, try the following home remedy for a moisturizer. My women patients love it because it makes their skin look and feel smooth, dewy, and youthful.

✚ DR. ORDON'S NATURAL MOISTURIZER

INGREDIENTS:

- ▫ 3 tablespoons of fresh cream
- ▫ ¼ avocado
- ▫ 1 tablespoon of honey

INSTRUCTIONS:

Place all three ingredients in a blender and puree into a smooth cream. Apply it to your skin, and let it remain on for at least an hour. Rinse it off with warm water. The fresh cream in this natural moisturizing cream provides your skin with vitamins and minerals that will keep it healthy and wrinkle-free. The avocado is rich in several fats and fat soluble vitamins that will fortify your skin and reduce the severity of existing wrinkles. Honey is a natural moisturizer and bacteria fighter.

Protect

About 20 to 30 years from now, maybe sooner, an awful lot of people are going to look like prunes overdone. Why? Because when they were in their teens or 20s, they periodically got themselves fried in tanning booths or out in the sun.

The sun barbecues and bastes our human hides during the summer months, relentlessly. Once, when I was young med school student, I plopped down on the beach and fell asleep in the sun for several hours, ignorant of what the Old Sol had in store for me. My poor, pale skin was baked to a color only slightly lighter than that of your average stop sign. Almost everything under the sun that you can squeeze from a tube was applied to my body in a futile attempt to relieve my discomfort.

I learned from that experience. Ever since then, I've avoided sun worshipping. I long ago conceded that I'd never become a bronze Greek god. Actually, getting tan would only have made me bronze; a Greek god and I are about as much alike as an elephant and an ant. But that's another story.

I believe if you're kind to your skin, it will serve you faithfully. My wife complains how much nicer my facial skin is than hers, although sometimes my skin is as pale as that of a corpse. But at least the sun's rays haven't boiled away its natural oils, and my skin is fairly moist.

Sunlight, artificial or natural, is your worst enemy, so proactive protection is key. The only true anti-wrinkle products are sunscreens. Apply sunscreen every time you leave the house. Sunscreen not only prevents future lines and wrinkles but may repair past damage. Look for ingredients like avobenzone, mexoryl, or zinc oxide that block the UVA rays, which are responsible for aging skin, or the words *"broad spectrum"* which means a sunscreen protects against both UVB and UVA rays.

Wear sunscreen even if you're not headed to the beach or spending the day outside because you get incidental sun exposure just walking to your mailbox, sitting at the bus stop, or doing errands. Even driving in your car can up your risk of sun damage. Studies looked at the complexions of people who spent a lot of time driving and found more sun damage on the left side of their faces than the right. I also tell my patients who run or jog to wear a hat with a visor to block the sun and, in really cold weather, a light face mask.

Apply sunscreen in wintertime too. While you're skiing, for example, the snow reflects the sun's rays and amplifies them up to 75 percent. And the higher the altitude, the greater the sun exposure. Look what happened to Robert Redford after years of Sundance.

Also, consider using a cream of green tea extract. It's a natural sun protectant. Research shows that natural ingredients in tea can reduce sun damage and may protect skin from skin cancer when applied topically. Using green tea extract may slow signs of aging and reduce sagging skin and wrinkles.

It's easy to whip up your own Green Tea Extract Cream at home.

✚ DR. ORDON'S GREEN TEA EXTRACT CREAM

INGREDIENTS:

- ☐ 3 green tea bags
- ☐ 1 mugful of water
- ☐ Container of shea butter (available at most local health food stores)

INSTRUCTIONS:

Microwave the tea bags in a mug of water for about 1 ½ minutes. Remove from the microwave and let the tea steep at room temperature for 1 hour.

Transfer the tea to a small saucepan. Squeeze out any water from tea bags into the sauce pan. Gently, at low temperature, boil down the tea, leaving a residue at the bottom of the pot, which is the extract.

Add the extract to ½ cup of the shea butter and mix until it becomes creamy. Refrigerate the mixture in a lidded container.

Smooth

Yes, anti-aging creams will smooth your skin, but you have to give them time to work their magic. It usually takes weeks of diligent use to reduce wrinkles. But natural remedies often get better results, thanks to fast-acting ingredients that work topically to relax or fill in lines in mere minutes. Use the following cream at night, and you'll see a subtle but noticeable softening of your wrinkles within a week of using it.

✚ DR. ORDON'S ANTI-AGING CREAM

INGREDIENTS:

▢ ½ cup of coconut oil

▢ 1 tablespoon of vitamin E oil

INSTRUCTIONS:

Mix both ingredients together and store in a jar at room temperature. Apply nightly at bed time. This is one of the best deep-wrinkle creams I've ever seen. You'll love the results.

If you don't want to mix up your own anti-aging cream, use one formulated with either alpha-lipoic acid, CoEnzyme Q-10 (CoQ-10), or an over-the-counter retinoid. Another good choice is Strivectin SD.

Alpha-lipoic acid is both water- and fat-soluble. That means it can better penetrate skin-cell membranes at all levels to protect them from free radicals, keeping the body and its skin strong. It can also erase fine lines and wrinkles, close up pores, and give your skin a healthy glow.

Your body naturally produces CoQ-10 to zap free radicals in cells, but as you age, the levels of CoQ-10 go down. This may make skin cells more susceptible to damage by free radicals and to wrinkles. This is why you see CoQ-10 as a wrinkle fighter in skin-care products such as toners, gels, and creams.

Retinoids such as Retin A and Renova have more than three decades worth of research behind them, which is why dermatologists and plastic surgeons consider them the gold standard as a topical wrinkle-fighting ingredient. They work by stimulating the skin's collagen producing cells—called *fibroblasts*—to make more collagen. As a result, skin is firmer, tighter, and smoother. Retinoids also speed up the skin's natural ability to slough off dead skin cells (also called *cell turnover*), which is something that slows down as you age.

Over-the-counter versions of retinoids are called *retinol* and are available at all price points from the drugstore versions to department and beauty-store products. Or you can see your dermatologist or plastic surgeon for a prescription like Retin-A and Renova, which contain higher concentrations of retinoids. If your skin is easily irritated by retinols, start by using a small amount every other day working up to daily use. If skin is still easily irritated, try a product with peptides, an ingredient made up of several amino acids that are believed to stimulate the production of collagen with less irritation. Use this on skin at night.

Originally a cream to reduce stretch marks on the body, StriVectin SD, with the help of Matrixyl, is now being used to diminish facial wrinkles. The product promises a smoother, younger complexion.

Age-Appropriate Skincare

AGE	CONDITION	TREATMENT RECOMMENDATIONS
20s	No visible wrinkling.	Use sunscreen religiously. Apply a moisturizer daily if your skin is dry.
30s	Fine lines may be developing and showing up as crow's-feet, frown lines, or smile lines.	Use sunscreen religiously. Apply a moisturizer daily if your skin is dry. Once daily, use an anti-wrinkle cream such as Strivectin or an antioxidant-based cream.
40s	Wrinkles may be obvious when your face is at rest, possibly a combination of normal aging and time spent in the sun.	Use sunscreen religiously. Apply a moisturizer daily if your skin is dry. Once daily, use an anti-wrinkle cream such as Strivectin or an antioxidant-based cream. Talk to your dermatologist or plastic surgeon about a prescription product such as Renova or Retin-A. Or use over-the-counter exfoliants such as hydroxyl acids.
50s	Wrinkles may be more deeply etched.	Use sunscreen religiously. Apply a moisturizer daily. Once daily, use an anti-wrinkle cream such as Strivectin or an antioxidant-based cream. Talk to your doctor about using a topical estrogen cream; it keeps skin taut, makes it naturally thicker, and arrests the development of further wrinkles. Consider a chemical peel or laser treatment to remove wrinkles. Look into injectable products such as Botox or crash fillers.

AGE	CONDITION	TREATMENT RECOMMENDATIONS
60s and beyond	You may have deep coarse wrinkling across your face, especially if you've had sun damage previously. To undo deep lines, you may have to consider more aggressive cosmetic procedures.	Use sunscreen religiously. Apply a moisturizer daily. Once daily, use an anti-wrinkle cream such as Strivectin or an antioxidant-based cream. Talk to your doctor about using a topical estrogen cream; it keeps skin taut, makes it naturally thicker, and arrests the development of further wrinkles. Look into treatments such as a deeper chemical peel or laser treatment or a face-lift.

Skin loves routine. Stick to this plan, and you'll see results in seven days. Then get into the habit of caring for your skin like this forever. Stick to the same products, too. If you're changing products all the time, your skin can get a little mad and react with irritation, redness, and more noticeable wrinkles.

Day 1

MORNING ROUTINE

Start the day with an acupressure massage. With firm pressure, use your middle and index fingers to massage several pressure points on your face using circular motions. This increases circulation and lymphatic drainage, which can give skin a youthful glow and a lift. Start by massaging the area between your brows with the fingers of one hand. Next, massage the skin above each eyebrow arch, followed by your temples. After this, continue your acupressure massage on the highest point of your cheekbones and then do so next to your nostrils. Lastly, with the middle and index fingers of one hand, massage the area right above the center of your upper lip and then the area right below the center of lower lip. Let each massage last about one minute. Do this when you wake up in the morning and repeat again before bed.

Enjoy my Wrinkle-Reducing Fruit Salad for breakfast. Take your supplements with breakfast.

Apply Green Tea Extract Cream to your skin underneath makeup with at least 30 SPF.

THROUGH THE DAY

Drink eight to ten glasses of water throughout the day.

At lunch or dinner, serve my Anti-wrinkle Mash.

Have a professional facial at a day spa to kick-start your anti-wrinkle program.

EVENING ROUTINE

Exfoliate your skin with my Sugar Facial Scrub.

Moisturize with my Natural Moisturizer.

Apply my Anti-aging Cream, or other recommended products, to your face prior to bedtime. Nighttime is really the best time to apply treatment products to your skin. You are going through a period of six, seven, or eight hours of sleep in which you're getting rest for yourself and are also resting your skin. During that time, your skin is not being exposed to sunlight, wind, sun, dirt, and other environmental elements that can break down any active ingredients. You're also moving around less, so products don't break down and stay put. Plus, your skin's temperature rises so it can better absorb moisturizers and active ingredients.

Day 2

MORNING ROUTINE

Start each day with an acupressure massage.

Enjoy my Wrinkle-Reducing Fruit Salad for breakfast. Take your supplements with breakfast.

Apply Green Tea Extract Cream to your skin underneath makeup with at least 30 SPF.

THROUGH THE DAY

Drink eight to ten glasses of water throughout the day.

At lunch or dinner, serve my Anti-Wrinkle Mash.

EVENING ROUTINE

Exfoliate your skin with my Sugar Facial Scrub.

Moisturize with my Natural Moisturizer.

Apply my Anti-aging Cream, or other recommended products, to your face prior to bedtime.

 Day 3

MORNING ROUTINE

Start the day with an acupressure massage.

Enjoy my Wrinkle-Reducing Fruit Salad for breakfast. Take your supplements with breakfast.

Apply Green Tea Extract Cream to your skin underneath makeup with at least 30 SPF.

THROUGH THE DAY

Drink eight to ten glasses of water throughout the day.

At lunch or dinner, serve my Anti-Wrinkle Mash.

EVENING ROUTINE

Apply my Seaweed Mask.

Moisturize with my Natural Moisturizer.

Apply my Anti-aging Cream, or other recommended products, to your face prior to bedtime.

 Day 4

MORNING ROUTINE

Start the day with an acupressure massage.

Enjoy my Wrinkle-Reducing Fruit Salad for breakfast. Take your supplements with breakfast.

Apply Green Tea Extract Cream to your skin underneath makeup with at least 30 SPF.

THROUGH THE DAY

Drink eight to ten glasses of water throughout the day.

At lunch or dinner, serve my Anti-wrinkle Mash.

EVENING ROUTINE

Exfoliate your skin with my Sugar Facial Scrub.

Moisturize with my Natural Moisturizer.

Apply my Anti-aging Cream, or other recommended products, to your face prior to bedtime.

Day 5

MORNING ROUTINE

Start the day with an acupressure massage.

Enjoy my Wrinkle-Reducing Fruit Salad for breakfast. Take your supplements with breakfast.

Apply Green Tea Extract Cream to your skin underneath makeup with at least 30 SPF.

THROUGH THE DAY

Drink eight to ten glasses of water throughout the day.

At lunch or dinner, serve my Anti-Wrinkle Mash.

EVENING ROUTINE

Exfoliate your skin with my Sugar Facial Scrub.

Moisturize with my Natural Moisturizer.

Apply my Anti-aging Cream, or other recommended products, to your face prior to bedtime.

Day 6

MORNING ROUTINE

Start the day with an acupressure massage.

Enjoy my Wrinkle-Reducing Fruit Salad for breakfast. Take your supplements with breakfast.

Apply Green Tea Extract Cream to your skin underneath makeup with at least 30 SPF.

THROUGH THE DAY

Drink eight to ten glasses of water throughout the day.

At lunch or dinner, serve my Anti-Wrinkle Mash.

EVENING ROUTINE

Exfoliate your skin with my Sugar Facial Scrub.

Moisturize with my Natural Moisturizer.

Apply my Anti-aging Cream, or other recommended products, to your face prior to bedtime.

 # Day 7

MORNING ROUTINE

Start the day with an acupressure massage.

Enjoy my Wrinkle-Reducing Fruit Salad for breakfast. Take your supplements with breakfast.

Apply Green Tea Extract Cream to your skin underneath makeup with at least 30 SPF

THROUGH THE DAY

Drink eight to ten glasses of water throughout the day.

At lunch or dinner, serve my Anti-Wrinkle Mash.

EVENING ROUTINE

Apply my Seaweed Mask.

Moisturize with my Natural Moisturizer.

Apply my Anti-aging Cream, or other recommended products, to your face prior to bedtime.

For some women, wrinkles just don't matter because they're comfortable with their looks and embrace the aging process. For others, wrinkles do matter because they want to look as youthful as they can for as long as they can. In my book, both attitudes are healthy.

If you're among those pursuing an anti-wrinkle program, the extra effort—and the benefits it brings—is well worth it, physically and emotionally. Just remember, though: Youthfulness is much more than just having a wrinkle-free complexion. It's a state of mind and spirit that never declines, even as time marches on.

 ASK DR. O

How long should you give an anti-wrinkle product to work?

Though we live in a fast-paced, I-want-it-now world, you need patience when it comes to your skin. Give a new product at least four to six weeks to work because it takes that long for cells to turn over and for skin to renew itself. Also, be consistent and follow directions exactly.

➡ QUICK TIPS TO FIGHT WRINKLES INSTANTLY

- ▫ **Tighten your skin naturally.** Twice a week, whip together the whites of two eggs. Then combine this with half a cup of mashed banana. Brush the banana/egg white mixture onto skin with a paintbrush and leave on for 15 to 20 minutes. Rinse well, pat skin dry, and apply your favorite moisturizer. The protein in egg helps nourish skin, and it also acts as an astringent to temporarily tighten skin. Nutrients in the banana like potassium, magnesium, phosphorus, and zinc help skin glow while the antioxidants it contains help protect it.

- ▫ **Always apply moisturizer to clean skin before makeup.** This fills in fine lines so makeup doesn't settle into them. (It also plumps up the skin so it looks smoother, at least temporarily.)

Let moisturizer absorb for three to five minutes.

- **Or use a makeup primer, which is a favorite makeup artist trick.** You know how you spackle a wall before painting it to fill in any cracks and holes? Makeup primer works the same way, filling in fine lines and wrinkles to create a smoother surface so makeup goes on better and doesn't highlight fine lines. Primer can also make pores look smaller.

- **Smooth on a light-reflecting foundation or tinted moisturizer.** When light bounces off the iridescent pigments that these products contain, it blurs fine lines, making them look less noticeable. Skin also looks more radiant. It's like your own personal lighting crew.

 ASK DR. O

I'm considering plastic surgery. What advice do you have?

I never want anyone to have regrets about a surgery or undergo ill-conceived procedures, so here are my top tips:

- Make sure you're not having plastic surgery for the wrong reasons. In other words, you're doing it because you want to do it, not because someone else (like your mother or a partner) is telling you to have plastic surgery.

- Have realistic expectations and goals. Don't seek out unrealistic results (for example, that you'll like a certain celebrity), and don't choose plastic surgery because you think that it will make all your problems go away. Yes, plastic surgery should make you feel better about yourself and make you feel more confident, but it won't change your life.

- Do your homework. Research the procedure(s) you're interested in and the doctor you're considering. Take your time, don't let cost be the determining factor, and when you meet with your surgeon, ask a lot of questions, like the following:

- Are you board certified by the American Board of Plastic Surgery?
- How often do you do the surgery I'm considering?
- Can I talk to some of your patients who have had this procedure?
- Can I see before and after photos of your work?

 ASK DR. O

Do at-home lasers really work?

Most of these new at-home devices are actually not lasers. They're light-emitting diodes (LEDs). If you stick with them, use them religiously, and give them at least a month or two to work, then you may see minimal to moderate improvement on fine lines. But they're not going to have much effect on truly deep lines.

better décolletage in 7

You might have gorgeous facial skin—tight, wrinkle-free, flawless—but a saggy, wrinkled, discolored chest. This is what happens when you fail to give your "décolletage" the same care as your face. *Décolletage*, a French word meaning "wearing a low-neck dress," is also the word we use to refer to this area; it includes the neck, cleavage, and shoulder areas.

The skin on the décolletage is one of the first places you tend to show your age, for two reasons. First, this area doesn't have as many oil glands, so it tends to dry out and look wrinkly. Second, décolletage has less elastic and thinner skin tissue than the face.

Women complain to me about their décolletage frequently. They dislike the wrinkles, crepey skin, hyperpigmentation, sun damage, freckles, or even that tattoo they should not have gotten. They want to feel better and more confident in dresses and tops that have low cuts, highlighting their cleavage, when they want to show a little more skin or wear a beautiful necklace.

In my office, I might use a fractional laser to treat wrinkles or age spots in this area, but this is a treatment that takes up to six sessions and can be pricey. Or I might use Botox, which is only temporary. But really, what is most important is to begin a regular skincare program to your décolletage just as you would your face. By doing so, you can do some serious smoothing and change the look of your décolletage rather dramatically.

Has your décolletage been over-exposed to the sun? Try the following test to find out. Slightly press your finger for a few seconds on the skin of your chest area. Lift your finger. If your skin shows a white spot that does not disappear right away, your skin is probably getting too much sun exposure. Cover up, use sunscreen, or seek shade, or all of the above. If you avoid excessive sun exposure, your skin in the décolletage area will stay young and healthy looking.

Also, start eating more nutritiously. I'm sounding like a broken record, but it bears repeating: Nutritious food provides the building blocks for healthy skin. Décolletage skin can be very sun-damaged. To help it heal, be sure to eat five or six servings of nonstarchy vegetables a day and four or five servings of fruit. Avoid trans fats (found in a lot of processed food garbage) and animal fats, and eat and cook with healthy oils like olive or walnut. Eat a serving of nuts, seeds, or beans every day.

Drink eight glasses of water every day, or at least enough to stay well hydrated. This will do as much to heal your damaged skin as skin care products will do. Flaxseed oil and borage oil supplements may help to repair skin as well, but talk with a physician before starting any supplement program.

Here's my seven-day program to start caring for your décolletage. Within a week, I can promise you that your décolleté skin will appear more youthful, firmer, and more radiant.

Day 1

MORNING ROUTINE

Gently scrub your décolletage with a loofah while showering or bathing to exfoliate your skin. Or use my Sugar Scrub on page 119. You can remedy this area enormously simply by exfoliating the skin. I wouldn't lie to you—it's true!

Next, apply an emollient such as jojoba oil, wheat germ oil, or a rich moisturizer while your skin is still wet to seal in moisture. Doing so replaces moisture and necessary skin lipids, which can be damaged by excessive sun exposure.

Dry your skin carefully by patting the area with a towel (don't rub).

Apply a specialty neck and décolleté cream afterward (available at most department stores).

This is very important: Apply a generous amount of sunscreen to the décolleté area 20 minutes prior to going outside, especially if you're wearing a low-cut outfit.

EVENING ROUTINE

Cleanse your décolletage with the same cleanser you use on your face. A nonsoap cleanser is best.

Apply a vitamin C cream prior to bedtime. Vitamin C removes dead protein cells without the harshness of peels. This cream can restore a smooth surface and a youthful glow to aging skin and is essential for the production of collagen. Vitamin C cream is perfect for treating the décolletage.

Wear Decollette Pads. These are adhesive-free patches of medical-grade silicone that are placed on the chest at night. They are the invention of an Emmy Award–winning makeup artist, who noticed that the silicone-based prosthetics she used on actors reduced wrinkles. You can find them online at *www.amazon.com*.

Sleep on your back instead of on your side. Sleeping is one of the leading causes of wrinkles, after the sun, and when you sleep on your side, you are ironing in wrinkles into your skin. When you sleep on your side, your breasts, because of their weight, fall together and create lines, wrinkles, and creases in the cleavage area, up the chest, and into your lower neck. If you have trouble sleeping on your back, try Vasseur Skincare's Beauty Pillow. It is specially designed to prevent wrinkles while you sleep.

Day 2

MORNING ROUTINE

Gently scrub your décolletage with a loofah while showering or bathing to exfoliate your skin. Or use my Sugar Scrub on page 119.

Next, apply an emollient such as jojoba oil, wheat germ oil, or a rich moisturizer while your skin is still wet, to seal in moisture.

Dry your skin carefully by patting the area with a towel (don't rub).

Rub fresh lemon or lime juice onto the area today; it acts as a natural alpha hydroxyl acid and is very effective at fighting freckles and age spots.

Apply a specialty neck and décolleté cream afterward.

Apply a generous amount of sunscreen to the décolleté area 20 minutes prior to going outside, especially if you are wearing a low-cut outfit.

EVENING ROUTINE

Cleanse your décolletage with the same cleanser you use on your face. A nonsoap cleanser is best.

Apply a vitamin C cream prior to bedtime.

Wear Decollette Pads while you sleep.

Sleep on your back instead of on your side.

Exercise your chest and back muscles regularly with the strength-training exercises I recommended on pages 32–34. They help build up the chest area and, in doing so, iron out wrinkly décolletage skin.

 Day 3

MORNING ROUTINE

Gently scrub your décolletage with a loofah while showering or bathing to exfoliate your skin. Or use my Sugar Scrub on page 119.

Next, apply an emollient such as jojoba oil, wheat germ oil, or a rich moisturizer while your skin is still wet, to seal in moisture.

Dry your skin carefully by patting the area with a towel (don't rub).

Apply a specialty neck and décolleté cream afterward.

Apply a generous amount of sunscreen to the décolleté area 20 minutes prior to going outside, especially if you are wearing a low-cut outfit.

EVENING ROUTINE

Cleanse your décolletage with the same cleanser you use on your face. A nonsoap cleanser is best.

Apply a vitamin C cream prior to bedtime.

Wear Decollette Pads while you sleep.

Sleep on your back instead of on your side.

Day 4

MORNING ROUTINE

Gently scrub your décolletage with a loofah while showering or bathing to exfoliate your skin. Or use my Sugar Scrub on page 119.

Next, apply an emollient such as jojoba oil, wheat germ oil, or a rich moisturizer while your skin is still wet, to seal in moisture.

Dry your skin carefully by patting the area with a towel (don't rub).

Rub fresh lemon or lime juice onto the area today; it acts as a natural alpha hydroxy acid and is very effective at fighting freckles and age spots.

Apply a specialty neck and décolleté cream afterward.

Apply a generous amount of sunscreen to the décolleté area 20 minutes prior to going outside, especially if you are wearing a low-cut outfit.

EVENING ROUTINE

Cleanse your décolletage with the same cleanser you use on your face. A nonsoap cleanser is best.

Apply a vitamin C cream prior to bedtime.

Wear Decollette Pads while you sleep.

Sleep on your back instead of on your side.

Exercise your chest and back muscles regularly with the strength-training exercises I recommended on pages 32–34. They help build up the chest area and, in doing so, iron out wrinkly décolletage skin.

 ## Day 5

MORNING ROUTINE

Gently scrub your décolletage with a loofah while showering or bathing to exfoliate your skin. Or use my Sugar Scrub on page 119.

Next, apply an emollient such as jojoba oil, wheat germ oil, or a rich moisturizer while your skin is still wet, to seal in moisture.

Dry your skin carefully by patting the area with a towel (don't rub).

Apply a specialty neck and décolleté cream afterward.

Apply a generous amount of sunscreen to the décolleté area 20 minutes prior to going outside, especially if you are wearing a low-cut outfit.

EVENING ROUTINE

Cleanse your décolletage with the same cleanser you use on your face. A nonsoap cleanser is best.

Apply a vitamin C cream prior to bedtime.

Wear Decollette Pads while you sleep.

Sleep on your back instead of on your side.

 ## Day 6

MORNING ROUTINE

Gently scrub your décolletage with a loofah while showering or bathing to exfoliate your skin. Or use my Sugar Scrub on page 119.

Next, apply an emollient such as jojoba oil, wheat germ oil, or a rich moisturizer while your skin is still wet, to seal in moisture.

Dry your skin carefully by patting the area with a towel (don't rub).

Rub fresh lemon or lime juice onto the area today; it acts as a natural alpha hydroxy acid and is very effective at fighting freckles and age spots.

Apply a specialty neck and décolleté cream afterward.

Apply a generous amount of sunscreen to the décolleté area 20 minutes prior to going outside, especially if you are wearing a low-cut outfit.

EVENING ROUTINE

Gently scrub your décolletage with a loofah while showering or bathing to exfoliate your skin. Or use my Sugar Scrub on page 119.

Apply a vitamin C cream prior to bedtime.

Wear Decollette Pads while you sleep.

Sleep on your back instead of on your side.

Exercise your chest and back muscles regularly with the strength-training exercises I recommended on pages 32–34.

 # Day 7

MORNING ROUTINE

Gently scrub your décolletage with a loofah while showering or bathing to exfoliate your skin. Or use my Sugar Scrub on page 119.

Next, apply an emollient such as jojoba oil, wheat germ oil, or a rich moisturizer while your skin is still wet, to seal in moisture.

Dry your skin carefully by patting the area with a towel (don't rub).

Rub fresh lemon or lime juice onto the area today; it acts as a natural alpha hydroxy acid and is very effective at fighting freckles and age spots.

Apply a specialty neck and décolleté cream afterward.

Apply a generous amount of sunscreen to the décolleté area 20 minutes prior to going outside, especially if you are wearing a low-cut outfit.

EVENING ROUTINE

If you're going out in the evening and wearing a low-cut top, fake flawlessness in one of two ways: One method is to spray your hands with a generous amount of leg make-up (in a tone that matches your décolleté area). Smear it over your décolletage, and let it dry. Then powder your chest. Another trick is to brush bronzer across the décolletage to conceal, followed by a subtle shimmer powder to reflect light.

Cleanse your décolletage with the same cleanser you use on your face. A nonsoap cleanser is best.

Apply a vitamin C cream prior to bedtime.

Wear Decollette Pads while you sleep.

Sleep on your back instead of on your side.

The bottom line is that it is never too late to reverse the effects of aging and sun damage on your décolletage. Taking care of your skin is a daily process, so starting today, treat your décolletage with the same care as your face, and you'll look younger in no time.

better your acne in 7

Just when you thought you'd never, ever see a zit again, those nasty eruptions pop up out of nowhere. There may not be a more horrifying moment than pimples erupting when you're a grown-up. My patients find their adult acne very cruel. Every time, they'll complain to me, "Why do I have to deal with wrinkles *and* zits?"

I tell them that *adult-onset acne*, as it is often called, is usually hormonally regulated. We know that it is caused by estrogen, progesterone, and testosterone, which all have an effect on the sebaceous glands (also called your *pores*), causing them to produce more pore-clogging oil. This is why acne is common during hormonal times like puberty, ovulation, menstruation, pregnancy, peri-menopause, and menopause. (Though sebaceous glands cover our bodies, we have more of them on the face and back, two areas where acne is most common.)

Acne is the number-one skin problem in the world, one that 54 percent of women older than 25 struggle with. And whether you break out as an adult has nothing to do with whether you had acne as a teenager. (One difference is that adult acne is usually on your chin and jaw line as opposed to teen acne, which typically appears on the nose, cheeks, and forehead.) Though blemishes take many forms (blackheads, whiteheads, red pimples, and under the skin bumps known as cystic acne), they all start in your sebaceous glands. These glands produce oil, known as *sebum*, and when they get clogged with that sebum along with dirt, makeup, and skin cells, a little abyss develops below the skin where bacteria can live, thrive, and cause pimples, cysts, and boils. Though it's still unclear why some people suffer from breakouts while others don't, genetics seem to play a role.

We don't know exactly why a lot of people get adult acne, but the idea that it is something that's confined to adolescence is a complete misnomer. Yes, teenage acne is more severe, but I can't tell my adult patients that their problem isn't serious. For them, it's something we think we should have been done with long, long ago.

The good news is that a lot can be done to alleviate zits from populating mature faces. I first tell my patients that they are not to blame. Nor is their diet. I tell my patients straight up—it wasn't eating too much chocolate, pizza, French fries, or having a dirty face that caused acne. A lot of that is just pure myth. There's just no clinical evidence to support it. Then I help them begin exploring medications and cosmetic procedures that can help.

I create specific regimens for my patients. Because each face is different, everyone responds to things differently, and sometimes we have to exercise a little patience finding the right treatment approach. Typically, when adult acne is the diagnosis, I might prescribe a combination of cleansers and topical serums with proven acne-fighting ingredients such as benzoyl peroxide and glycolic acid. The drugs Renova and topical Retin-A (both available by prescription) achieve great results for many patients. Plus, there's a bonus: both are potent weapons in smoothing fine lines. So, there's a double whammy: we're getting rid and acne and wrinkles at the same time.

The most potent treatment for severe acne is Accutane, a vitamin-A derivative that's highly effective against severe, persistent, cystic acne. The results are nothing short of miraculous. But there's a huge downside; it is devastatingly dangerous for women who conceive while taking it. The drug causes birth defects.

There are several home remedies you can use to treat acne, without resorting to possibly dangerous drugs. I've listed these remedies in the coming sections, and they're incorporated in my seven-day plan.

✚ DR. ORDON'S BASIL TONER

INGREDIENTS:

- 3 tablespoons of dried basil leaves
- 1 cup of boiling water

DIRECTIONS:

Crush up the dried basil leaves and mix them into a cup of boiling water. Once the mixture cools, strain out the basil leaves, put it in a spray bottle, and spritz your skin. Use a cotton ball or pad to spread toner gently around your face. Do this daily before cleansing. Basil acts as an antiseptic, helps get rid of bacteria, and improves circulation to skin.

✚ DR. ORDON'S EASY-CARE ACNE TREATMENT #1

INGREDIENTS:

- 2 baby aspirins
- Water

DIRECTIONS:

Take two baby aspirin, put them in a plastic bag, and mash them up. Then add a little bit of water to form a paste and apply this paste directly to your blemish. Cover the area with a Band-Aid for ten minutes to help the aspirin penetrate skin better. Aspirin contains salicylic acid, a compound found in many topical acne medications. It works by helping slough off the top layer of dead skin cells faster, cleaning out the pores and neutralizing the bacteria inside those pores.

✚ DR. ORDON'S EASY-CARE ACNE TREATMENT #2

INGREDIENTS:

- ☐ Brewer's Yeast
- ☐ A squeeze of lemon juice
- ☐ Water

DIRECTIONS:

I learned this at-home remedy from beauty expert Kym Douglas during one of her many visits to *The Doctors* green room. Make a paste using a little bit of brewer's yeast, a squeeze of lemon juice, and bit of water. Apply this paste right on your blemish, and leave it on for ten minutes. Just like you can do with the aspirin remedy, cover the area with a Band-Aid. The brewer's yeast fights bacteria, and the lemon helps dry the blemish. Choose one of these recipes or alternate on different days (just don't do one after the other or on the same day). And always make sure your skin is cleansed first.

Also, there are some important general recommendations you should follow to get clear, unblemished skin.

Cleanse Right

Washing your face is one of the keys to a clear complexion because it removes the oil, dirt, and bacteria that can clog pores. But harshly rubbing your skin won't help. Here are some do's and don'ts for cleansing:

- ☐ Don't over-scrub, especially with abrasive cleansers, soaps, or products that contain alcohol. Rough treatment can irritate existing acne and cause inflammation, which only makes your breakouts worse.

- ☐ Do wash with a cleanser that contains salicylic acid or benzoyl peroxide. Salicylic acid is a beta hydroxy acid that helps soak up oils on the skin's surface and unclog pores. Benzoyl peroxide dries up pimples, reduces bacteria, and cleans pores.

☐ Don't over-cleanse. Often people with acne think that their skin is dirty and that washing it as much as possible will help. The truth is that washing any more than twice a day can strip the skin of its natural oils. As a result, one of two things can happen. By dehydrating the skin, there can actually be a rebound effect where the skin produces more oil to compensate for what you've taken away. Or skin gets so dry and chapped that dry flakes can clog pores.

☐ Do wet skin before applying your cleanser. Many women put cleanser directly on their skin. But unless the label says otherwise, most cleanser's ingredients are activated when combined with water.

☐ Don't use a washcloth, puff, pouf, or any other scrubbing tool to apply cleanser to your face. Instead, massage it onto wet skin with your hands using a light touch. "Light" is the key word here since being too rough can irritate skin, worsen breakouts, and make them last longer.

☐ Don't wash skin with steaming hot water. Steam and heat are known to open pores, so this may seem like a good idea. But water that's too hot can strip, irritate, and inflame skin. Instead, wash up with lukewarm water.

☐ Do rinse skin completely so there's no irritating residue left behind. Splash your face at least ten times, and don't forget the sides of the face, neck, and ears where cleanser can migrate.

Stop Drying Your Skin with Towels

Stock up on tissues for these seven days and use them to gently pat your complexion after washing, leaving skin slightly damp. Using a tissue guarantees that you're drying your face with something clean each time as opposed to using a bathroom towel that's used over and over (by you or other people) and may harbor dirt or bacteria. Plus, a tissue's surface is gentler on skin than a towel's.

Look at Your Makeup

Often women with acne apply extra makeup to skin so they can cover their blemishes and make skin look better. But this creates a vicious cycle because makeup and certain cosmetics can plug pores even more and a condition called *acne cosmetica* where skincare, makeup, and hair styling products cause mild bumps and breakouts. Make sure that all products you use say that they're "noncomedogenic," which means they won't clog pores.

Check for Friction

Acne mechanica is the formal name for blemishes caused by repetitive motion against the skin. Things that are used or worn for long periods of time typically cause this type of acne. These include straps from bike helmets, bags or backpacks, hats, tight clothing, bra straps, headbands, musical instruments, or even resting your face in your hands frequently.

Watch Your Diet

Anecdotal evidence has found that when acne-prone people who were consuming a lot of soy foods stopped eating them, their acne improved. More research needs to be done, but this may be because soy has a hormonal effect on the body. Other research shows a link between breakouts and dairy (especially milk products) and that limiting them can help clear up your complexion. One theory here is that hormones found in milk products may be to blame. For the next seven days, limit your dairy and soy intake to see whether this makes a difference.

Additionally, eat foods rich in omega-3 fatty acids daily to hydrate skin from within and help reduce inflammation. Good options include salmon, flaxseeds, flaxseed oil, walnuts, and fish oil supplements.

Eat at least one tablespoon of olive oil daily. It contains compounds called polyphenols, which are said to prevent skin discoloration caused by acne and reduce inflammation.

Keep Your Hands to Yourself

You may be touching your face hundreds of times during the day without realizing it and unintentionally depositing dirt and bacteria on your skin. Have a hands-off policy when it comes to your face, touching it only when cleansing. (And make sure to wash your hands before cleaning skin.) Try to apply products and makeup with tools like cotton swabs, clean makeup brushes, or clean wands to minimize hand to face contact—and the pimples that may come with it. Also, buttons in public places like elevators, ATMs, and exercise machines at the gym can harbor germs. If possible, use your knuckle not the pad of your finger to press them since your knuckles rarely touch your face.

Rethink Facial Hair Removal

Waxing, tweezing, and hair removal creams known as depilatories work well for removing facial hair. But they can also cause breakouts for some people by pushing bacteria, dirt, and dead skin cells deeper into your sebaceous glands. To prevent this, cleanse skin with your antiacne wash right before you remove hair. Then apply an over-the-counter antibiotic to the area to reduce the amount of bacteria on your skin.

Manage Stress

When you're stressed, your skin produces the hormone cortisol. This can happen whether your stress is good (you're getting married, going on vacation, or interviewing for a great job) or bad (like a demanding deadline at work or a fight with a partner). High levels of cortisol can lead to inflammation and slow down the skin's ability to heal your acne.

Change How You Style Your Hair

Often acne along the hairline, sides of the face, and forehead is caused by hair styling products that get onto skin when you're doing your hair or migrate there during the day. These products often contain heavy oils or ingredients that can clog the pores. This condition is so common that there's actually a name for it: pomade acne. For these seven days, you have two options.

The first: don't use your hair products at all. This alone can clear up your skin.

If that's not possible, apply products to hair more carefully.

Put them on your hands and then your hair rather than spraying them directly onto your hair (and potentially your skin).

Apply product a few inches away from the hairline so they can't move onto skin as easily.

Once you're done doing your hair, take a facial wipe or moistened cotton pad and gently wipe the skin along your hairline, forehead and sides of the face.

If you exercise during the day, pull your hair off and away from your face to decrease the chances that sweating will cause your hair products to move onto your skin.

Visualize Better Skin

Close your eyes for a few minutes a day, and imagine yourself with clearer skin. It may sound a little bit hokey, but visualization and a positive attitude may improve your complexion.

Day 1

Prep your skin with my Basil Toner.

If you have any whiteheads, do the following: place a warm compress on the pimple for a few minutes, followed by a cooled chamomile tea bag. This reduces inflammation, opens the pimple up, and has a bacteriostatic effect so it will kill some of the bacteria inside the sebaceous gland.

Apply a treatment product. These are available over-the-counter with ingredients like salicylic acid, benzoyl peroxide, and retinoic acid, which exfoliate the dead skin cells on the uppermost layer of the skin to help heal blemishes. Or use one of the Easy-Care Acne Treatments.

Wash all your makeup brushes and applicators. This removes any dirt, oil, and bacteria in their bristles that can contaminate your skin each time you use them. Makeup artists say that natural bristle brushes apply makeup better, but they also retain skin's oils and bacteria more than the synthetic variety. To clean them, blend a tablespoon of baby shampoo with a half-teaspoon tea tree oil in a small dish. Wet your makeup brush (only from the bristles down, not the metal or handle of the brush), swish the bristles in the shampoo/tea tree oil mixture for a minute, and then rinse thoroughly with lukewarm water. Place your brush on the edge of a countertop with the bristles hanging off to make sure it dries completely before using it again. (Don't put your brush in an enclosed area like a cabinet or drawer to dry because the darkness combined with the water can cause bacteria to grow.) Also, replace any makeup sponges with new ones.

Clean your cell phone daily. Think about the places your phone has been over the course of a day: your desk, car, bathroom sink, and the coffee bar at Starbucks, among others. In each of these places your phone can pick up dirt, bacteria, and other debris, which can irritate and worsen acne-prone skin when you put your phone up to your face. Disinfect your phone daily using an alcohol wipe. You can also get a headset to keep your phone away from your skin altogether.

Change your pillow case daily for the next seven days. This keeps bacteria, dirt, and hair styling products from your pillow case away from your skin. Also, sleep on your back so that no area of your face comes in contact with your sheets, and pull your hair back and away from your face while you sleep. Besides keeping potential irritants from your pillowcase away from your skin, sleeping on your back will keep your nighttime acne treatment product from rubbing off.

Moisturize your skin. It may seem counterintuitive to add moisture to oily skin, but ingredients in many acne products, like those that contain retinoids and salicylic acid, can really dry skin out (especially in the beginning before skin is acclimated to the product), so a moisturizer is needed to hydrate and soothe. Also, very dry skin can be acne-prone because chapped, dry flakes can clog pores. Look for oil-free moisturizers that don't contain mineral oil, shea butter, and petrolatum. These ingredients may clog pores and, because they create a film layer on the skin, block the absorption of acne fighting ingredients that you apply after moisturizing.

➡ BETTER ON THE SPOT

While you wait for skin to clear up, here's how to make a blemish less noticeable.

Place an ice cube on the pimple for one to two minutes. This reduces inflammation and enhances the absorption of the products you'll put on the skin next.

Apply a few drops of Visine to the pimple. This is an old, Hollywood makeup artist trick because these over-the-counter eye drops contain tetrahydrozoline hydrochloride, an ingredient that's a vasoconstrictor. This means it constricts blood vessels and, as a result, helps reduce the pimple's redness and inflammation.

Let this dry for a minute and then dab on a spot treatment pimple product that contains benzoyl peroxide. Wait a few minutes before putting on any makeup.

If you wear foundation or tinted moisturizer, apply it to your face as usual. This may be all you need to minimize the appearance of your blemish.

If you think you need more coverage, blend two shades of creamy concealer—one that matches your skin tone and one that's one shade darker. Use a pointed concealer brush to gently apply to your blemish and blend lightly your ring finger, which isn't as strong as the rest of your fingers so it gives a lighter touch, or a brush. For a larger, red blemish, look for color correction makeup in a green shade to neutralize its reddish/pink color.

Apply a dab of powder on top of this with a brush to help your cover up stay put.

When it comes to covering up breakouts, less is more. In other words, don't pile a pimple with makeup because then you're just trading one problem (a zit) for another (makeup that looks caked on and draws more attention).

➡ THE FINAL ANSWER ON...PIMPLE POPPING

To pop or not to pop? That is the question. The answer? Don't do it, no matter how tempted you are! It may seem like squeezing a pimple, especially a blackhead or pus-filled white head, would help it look better and heal faster. But the opposite is actually true. Squeezing and digging into skin with your fingernails can push dirt, oil, and bacteria further into the pimple, and you can form what we call an *excoriation*, which is an injury to the skin. This can lead to an infection, scabbing, and scarring.

 # Day 2

Prep your skin with my Basil Toner.

Treat any whiteheads, as described earlier.

Apply a treatment product.

Clean your cell phone.

Change your pillow case.

Exfoliate your skin today get rid of potentially pore clogging, dead cells. There are two types of exfoliating products. Chemical exfoliators use chemical ingredients like salicylic acid to loosen dead cells from the skin's surface. Physical exfoliators manually remove these cells with things like beads, crushed shells, or the bumpy surface of a facial puff. Either one works; just choose one that's oil-free and made for acne-prone skin. And if you choose a physical exfoliator, make sure it's made of beads and not of crushed shells, fruit seeds, or nuts, which can irritate existing acne and tear skin with their uneven edges.

Moisturize your skin.

 # Day 3

Prep your skin with my Basil Toner.

Treat any whiteheads, as described earlier.

Apply a treatment product.

Clean your cell phone.

Change your pillow case.

Moisturize your skin.

 ASK DR. O

Can the sun clear acne up my acne?

The answer is yes and no. Initially, the sun may dry up your blemishes. But it can actually worsen breakouts by causing inflammation and irritation. Plus, UV rays can darken the marks often left behind after a blemish heals (called *post-inflammatory hyperpigmentation*) and make them last longer. The key is to protect skin from the sun without using a sunscreen that causes more breakouts.

Make sure to choose a product labeled "oil free" and "noncomedogenic."

Opt for sunscreen that contains physical sunblock ingredients rather than chemical ones. Physical sunscreens, which include zinc oxide and titanium dioxide, create a protective barrier by staying on the skin's surface. On the other hand, chemical sunscreens, which include avobenzone (Parsol 1789), oxybenzone, methoxycinnamate, and octocylene, protect by being absorbed into the skin, which can be more irritating.

Gel sunscreen formulations are a great option for acne-prone skin because they're less oily than thick creams or lotions. Or try mineral-based powdered sunscreens, which you dust on skin like makeup. They're good for sensitive or acne prone complexions because they're lightweight, soak up excess oil, reduce the appearance of redness, and protect against the sun's dangerous rays with physical sunscreens like titanium dioxide and zinc oxide.

Apply sunscreen to freshly cleansed skin so you don't trap dirt and oil in your pores.

You need more than sunscreen to avoid the sun's rays. Wear a broad-brimmed hat and sunglasses, and stay in the shade as much as possible, especially during the hours of 10 a.m. and 4 p.m. when those UV rays are the strongest.

Wash your face well at night to make sure you don't go to sleep with pore-clogging sunscreen residue on your skin.

 # Day 4

Prep your skin with my Basil Toner.

Treat any whiteheads, as described earlier.

Apply a treatment product.

Clean your cell phone.

Change your pillow case.

Moisturize your skin.

 ## FACT OR FICTION?

A dab of toothpaste can clear up a pimple.
Fiction. This may have been true years ago when toothpastes contained fewer ingredients. But the fluoride, whitening, and tartar-reducing ingredients in modern-day products can actually irritate and inflame skin, making a pimple or blemish even worse. Bottom line: save your toothpaste for your teeth!

 ## FACT OR FICTION?

Putting glue on your blackheads is an at-home version of blackhead removal strips.

Fiction. Patients ask me about all sorts of crazy things and this is one of them. I guess there's a rumor out there that you can apply glue to your skin and rip it off when it dries and clean out your pores. Though you may lift some oil off the skin's surface, it's doubtful that you'll eliminate your blackheads. Instead, you may cause redness and skin irritation.

📅 Day 5

Prep your skin with my Basil Toner.

Treat any whiteheads, as described earlier.

Apply a treatment product.

Clean your cell phone.

Change your pillow case.

Exfoliate your skin today.

Moisturize your skin.

➡ THE DOCTOR WILL SEE YOU NOW...

If over-the-counter remedies don't work, make an appointment with a dermatologist to discuss other options. These include the following:

- Prescription topical medications have higher strengths of ingredients like benzoyl peroxide, retinoids, and salicylic acid than over-the-counter products. Once you and your doctor find a medication that works, it's important to use it on the entire acne-prone area (not just the few pimples you see at the moment) and to continue using it even after skin clears to prevent future breakouts.

- Oral birth control pills. Like I mentioned earlier, acne can be hormonally regulated, so oral birth control pills work by stabilizing your hormone levels. Several brands have been FDA-approved to control acne, which they do by regulating the production of excess oil.

- Doctor's office procedures that include blue light therapy, infrared light therapy, photodynamic therapy, and intense pulsed light laser combined with a gentle vacuum may be the miracle cure for even the most stubborn cases of acne. These don't guarantee clearer skin, but they may help especially in conjunction with the use of the right cleansers and spot treatment products at home. Some of these doctor's office procedures like blue light therapy have been shown to clear skin by 30 percent to 60 percent, according to the American Academy of Dermatology.

They typically require a series of treatments spaced about a week apart, and their fees are not always covered by insurance. For more information, talk to a board-certified dermatologist.

Day 6

Prep your skin with my Basil Toner.

Treat any whiteheads, as described earlier.

Apply a treatment product.

Clean your cell phone.

Change your pillow case.

Moisturize your skin.

 SEE YOUR M.D. ASAP

If you're experiencing unexplained weight gain, excessive hair growth on your face or breasts, an irregular menstrual cycle, and difficulty conceiving along with your blemishes, the cause may be polycystic ovary disease. This is a condition where your hormones are out of balance, so it's important to get a doctor's diagnosis and treatment.

Day 7

Prep your skin with my Basil Toner.

Treat any whiteheads, as described earlier.

Apply a treatment product.

Clean your cell phone.

Change your pillow case.

Exfoliate your skin today.

Moisturize your skin.

Have you ever noticed that often after a pimple heals, it leaves a dark spot or patch of pigment in its wake? This is a condition called *post-inflammatory hyperpigmentation* and happens because your body sees the skin inflammation and pimple as an injury. As a result, pigment-making cells are stimulated. This can happen from over-drying a pimple, which irritates the skin, or from picking or popping it. This is especially a problem in ethnic skin, which contains more pigment. That's just another reason not to pick, pop, or aggravate a pimple!

younger hands in 7

They're a dead giveaway of your age.

I'm not talking about crow's-feet, marionette lines, or a turkey neck.

I'm talking about your hands.

Take a look. Maybe you've got brown spots from your days in the sun or your skin isn't as tight as it used to be. Perhaps you've got bulging veins atop thin, wrinkly skin. Your hands just don't look as pretty as they used to.

But does it even matter? Sure it does. Think about it. When you shake someone's hand, rest your hands on the table, run your fingers through your hair, or simply raise a glass to your lips...your hands will get noticed.

A lot of women are now getting embarrassed by their telltale, aging hands, which is why in plastic surgery and cosmetics, there's a lot of attention focused on hands.

In my practice, I might use chemical peels to help repair the skin and restore more even pigmentation. Another trend is volume replacement, which might be used along with a chemical peel. This procedure involves injecting the hands with various types of plump-up products. One is hyaluronic acid, a substance found naturally in the body that stimulates skin cells weight loss to increase the production of collagen and elastin so that the hand's skin looks plump and youthful. The results usually last 6 to 12 months.

Another technique is to use the patient's own fat. I harvest a small amount of fat from areas such as the inner thighs, abdomen, or knees. The fat is processed and centrifuged and then immediately injected into the hands. You have to wear bandages for a few days after the procedure, and there may be some bruising. However, once this has cleared, your hands look plump and rejuvenated.

As with any procedure involving the patient's own fat, the body may metabolize it quickly, and therefore it's tough to predict how long the effects will last. You might need a second session, but the results from this procedure can sometimes last for years.

There are other ways to attack the problem of aging hands naturally—methods that work pretty quickly and will keep your hands soft and young-looking, without going to the extremes of a cosmetic procedure. Here is some important general advice.

Give Hands a Seaweed Treatment

Seaweed is rich in nourishing vitamins, important minerals, such as potassium, calcium, magnesium, phosphorus, iron, zinc, and manganese, and nutrients, such as folic acid and niacin. It's also a great exfoliator helping to loosen and remove dead skin cells and dry flakes. At the same time, it provides hydration to the skin. Here's my Seaweed Treatment for Hands.

✚ DR. ORDON'S SEAWEED TREATMENT FOR HANDS

MATERIALS:

- ☐ Sheets of seaweed (called *nori* and available in the ethnic aisle of many supermarkets or health food stores)
- ☐ Water

DIRECTIONS:

Place two to three sheets of seaweed in a pot of boiling water. Turn off the heat and allow seaweed to soften. Gently remove it from the pot, letting it cool off so it's not boiling, and then place strips of warm, cooked seaweed on the backs of your hands for 5 to 10 minutes. Then, over a sink rub seaweed around your fingers and hands like you do when washing up with soap for 15 to 20 seconds. Rinse thoroughly.

Fade Your Brown Spots

These spots are the results of damage to the melanocytes—the cells that produce the dark pigment responsible for the color of our skin and hair (melanin). When you're in your 20s and early 30s, and the melanocytes do their job normally. They produce nice, even pigment that covers your skin uniformly. But with too much unprotected sun exposure, the melanocytes begin to produce pigment erratically, resulting in a patchy appearance.

Regularly exfoliating your hands can lift off the top layer of dead skin cells, which contain some of the pigment that's leaving spots. "Age Spots Be-Gone" is my favorite natural remedy.

✚ DR. ORDON'S AGE SPOTS BE-GONE

INGREDIENTS:

- ☐ ½ cup uncooked brown rice
- ☐ 1 tablespoon agave nectar
- ☐ 1 tablespoon lemon juice

DIRECTIONS:

Mix together the above ingredients and blend well. Apply the mixture to dry hands. Move the scrub around your hands in circular motions on the backs of hands with firm but gentle pressure for one to two minutes. You can also rub this rice scrub on the palms of the hands to soften calluses. The rice exfoliates, the agave hydrates, and the lemon helps lighten skin and lift off dead cells.

Soften Hands Naturally

I've cooked up two amazing remedies that will leave your hands feeling silky smooth: my Cinnamon Hand Soak and my Nighttime Hand Moisturizer.

✚ DR. ORDON'S CINNAMON HAND SOAK

INGREDIENTS:

- ☐ 2 cups of water
- ☐ 1 cup of milk
- ☐ 1 ½ tablespoons of olive oil
- ☐ 1 pinch of ground cinnamon

DIRECTIONS:

Mix all the ingredients in a microwaveable bowl that has enough room to fit both hands in. Place the bowl in the microwave for about 20 seconds or until it feels warm enough. But not piping hot, please!

Soak your hands in the mixture for about ten minutes. Then, rinse your hands with lukewarm water and pat dry. You can apply your favorite hand moisturizer to top off the soak.

✚ DR. ORDON'S NIGHTTIME HAND MOISTURIZER

INSTRUCTIONS:

At night, apply a thick layer of vegetable shortening to the fronts and backs of your hands. Cover them with a pair of thick, cotton socks and sleep this way. Vegetable shortening is made from oils like soybean and cotton seed oil that have been chemically altered and turned into a solid form. The fat that it contains may not be good for the heart, but it's great for softening the skin and alleviating dryness and itchiness. Plus, the heat your body generates beneath the socks or gloves while you sleep helps it better penetrate the skin. In the morning, towel off any excess. (This is great for rough feet, too.)

Create a Barrier Between Your Skin and Harsh Chemicals

It's tough to avoid harsh detergents and chemicals during the day, including soap, household cleansers, bleach, laundry detergent, and all the anti-bacterial products that are so popular today. On top of this, cleaning and caretaking often requires submerging your hands in water for long periods of time, which washes away the skin's natural oils known as *sebum*. So, unless you can convince someone else to do all the cleaning and laundry in your home, wear gloves while you clean, do dishes, or handle any other chemicals like at-home hair color.

Ditch the Soap

Soap can strip skin of natural oils leaving hands dry and itchy and nails brittle. Instead, wash your hands with a soap-free hydrating cleanser. Or try one that doesn't require water. These products are designed to be removed with a tissue so that hands get clean, but they leave a layer of moisturizers behind.

Skip the Hand Sanitizers

Anti-bacterial products are more popular than ever. But experts believe you don't really need to use them to prevent germs and that, in fact, overuse of these products is why some antibiotic-resistant bacteria exist. Also, many of these products contain alcohol and an anti-bacterial ingredient called *triclosan* that is extremely drying and irritating to skin. To avoid germs, simply wash hands often. If you want to use hand sanitizers, choose one that's triclosan-free.

Quit Cracking Your Knuckles

Your mother was right when she told you that chronically cracking your knuckles could make them bigger. It can also cause wrinkles. While you're trying to break this habit, find other things you can do in place of knuckle cracking such as squeezing silly putty, stress balls, and Play-Doh.

Now on to my seven-day plan for better, more youthful hands.

 # Day 1

MORNING ROUTINE

Keep your bath or shower short. Use lukewarm water; hot water causes natural oils and moisture to evaporate from your skin, just what you want to avoid.

Blot your hands dry. Vigorous rubbing creates tiny tears in the skin, leading to rough, chapped, dry hands.

Apply a moisturizer formulated for hands. A good one is StriVectin-HC Ultra-Concentrate Cream For The Hands. It helps improves the appearance of age spots and unsightly discolorations and restores youthful texture, tone, and firmness to the skin of your hands.

Protect your hands from the sun by using a good sun-protection product with an SPF of at least 30. Also, wear gloves when you're out in extremely cold weather or wind because these things can dry skin and cause painful cracks.

THROUGH THE DAY

Make a habit of applying cream to your hands several times during the day. Carry small tubes of moisturizers in your pocket or purse to use when away from home. If in your daily work, your hands constantly get wet (think: doctors, nurses, dentists, beauticians, housekeepers, parents, and many others), so keep a bottle of moisturizer handy and use it often.

EVENING ROUTINE

Give your hands my Age Spots Be-Gone treatment.

Apply my Nighttime Hand Moisturizer as directed.

 # Day 2

MORNING ROUTINE

Keep your bath or shower short. Use lukewarm water; hot water depletes moisture from hands.

Blot your hands dry.

Treat your hands to my Seaweed Treatment today.

Apply a moisturizer formulated for hands.

Protect your hands from the sun by using a good sun-protection product with an SPF of at least 30. Also, wear gloves when you're out in extremely cold weather.

THROUGH THE DAY

Apply cream to your hands several times during the day.

EVENING ROUTINE

Give your hands my Age Spots Be-Gone treatment.

Apply my Nighttime Hand Moisturizer as directed.

 # Day 3

MORNING ROUTINE

Keep your bath or shower short. Use lukewarm water; hot water depletes moisture from hands.

Blot your hands dry.

Apply a moisturizer formulated for hands.

Protect your hands from the sun by using a good sun-protection product with an SPF of at least 30. Also, wear gloves when you're out in extremely cold weather.

Apply cream to your hands several times during the day.

EVENING ROUTINE

Apply my Nighttime Hand Moisturizer as directed.

 # Day 4

MORNING ROUTINE

Keep your bath or shower short. Use lukewarm water; hot water depletes moisture from hands.

Blot your hands dry.

Treat your hands to my Seaweed Treatment today.

Apply a moisturizer formulated for hands.

Protect your hands from the sun by using a good sun-protection product with an SPF of at least 30. Also, wear gloves when you're out in extremely cold weather.

THROUGH THE DAY

Apply cream to your hands several times during the day.

EVENING ROUTINE

Give your hands my Age Spots Be-Gone treatment.

Apply my Nighttime Hand Moisturizer as directed.

 # Day 5

MORNING ROUTINE

Keep your bath or shower short. Use lukewarm water; hot water depletes moisture from hands.

Blot your hands dry.

Apply a moisturizer formulated for hands.

Protect your hands from the sun by using a good sun-protection product with an SPF of at least 30. Also, wear gloves when you're out in extremely cold weather.

THROUGH THE DAY
Apply cream to your hands several times during the day.

EVENING ROUTINE
Apply my Nighttime Hand Moisturizer as directed.

 # Day 6

MORNING ROUTINE
Keep your bath or shower short. Use lukewarm water; hot water depletes moisture from hands.

Blot your hands dry.

Treat your hands to my Seaweed Treatment today.

Apply a moisturizer formulated for hands.

Protect your hands from the sun by using a good sun-protection product with an SPF of at least 30. Also, wear gloves when you're out in extremely cold weather.

THROUGH THE DAY
Apply cream to your hands several times during the day.

EVENING ROUTINE
Give your hands my Age Spots Be-Gone treatment.

Apply my Nighttime Hand Moisturizer as directed.

 # Day 7

MORNING ROUTINE
Keep your bath or shower short. Use lukewarm water; hot water depletes moisture from hands.

Blot your hands dry.

Apply a moisturizer formulated for hands.

Protect your hands from the sun by using a good sun-protection product with an SPF of at least 30. Also, wear gloves when you're out in extremely cold weather.

THROUGH THE DAY

Apply cream to your hands several times during the day.

EVENING ROUTINE

Apply my Nighttime Hand Moisturizer as directed.

The aging process affects your whole body, not just the face. Although we often invest the most in our face in terms of aesthetic procedures, the rest of the body also needs regular attention, including your hard-working hands.

better nails in 7

Why is it so hard to grow and maintain lovely, long, hard nails? Well, the main reason is that nails aren't alive; they're dead. If they were living tissue, they could heal themselves instead of making us do it for them. Next question: If nails are dead, how do they grow? Actually, they don't; new cells, which develop deep under your cuticles, push out the older, dead ones, forming those nails women love to polish. Here's how to have yours looking great in no time.

My Cuticle Citrus Treatment

Got ragged cuticles? Give them my citrus treatment. The purpose of the cuticle is to protect the nail and keep bacteria out of the body. Cutting them can lead to redness, swelling, and even an infection, all of which can be painful.

STEP 1

Cut a grapefruit in half horizontally so that its triangle sections are exposed, and remove any seeds. Apply a drop of vitamin E oil or olive oil to each cuticle. Then submerge your nails into the flesh of the grapefruit, one finger per section for two to three minutes. (Don't do this if cuticles are cut, red, or irritated.) Submerging your nails in the grapefruit exfoliates and softens cuticles so they're ready for step 2.

STEP 2

Rinse your hands completely of any grapefruit juice. Cover one index finger with a soft cloth, and use light pressure to push small sections of the cuticle back at a time. If you have a dangling piece of cuticle that you really want to remove, do so with a sterile nail scissors or cuticle clipper and cut the dead skin very gently without tugging or pulling.

STEP 3

Soothe inflamed cuticles. If cuticles and/or the surrounding skin are red and irritated, you can get some relief by soaking nails in a cup of full-fat, plain yogurt that has been chilled in the freezer for five to ten minutes and then sprinkled with one teaspoon of cinnamon. The yogurt's cool temperature and fat quiets inflamed skin, and the lactic acid exfoliates while the antimicrobial benefits of cinnamon help prevent infection. This yogurt soak also softens skin, so it's a good way to prepare cuticles to gently push them back.

Stop Biting Your Nails

Nail biting is a bad habit, for several reasons. The first is aesthetic. Chewed-up nails and cuticles aren't pretty. More importantly, tearing your cuticles with your teeth allows infection-causing bacteria to enter the body. Also, unless you wash your hands well before you start biting, your fingers probably have germs on them that can make you sick. (Just think of all the things your hands touch in a day that may harbor other people's germs and bacteria like money, ATM machine buttons, pens, and subway or bus handles and stair railings, among others.) You can kick this habit with an anti-nibbling polish. Their horrible taste—sort of bitter and chemical—is supposed to make nails less tempting. Regular at-home or professional manicures may also help because not only are you getting rid of the things that are so enticing to bite like hangnails, jagged cuticles, and rough-edged nails, but you're spending time and money that you may not want to waste. Always carry a nail file and cuticle nipper with you on the go so you can properly cut anything that you'd typically bite. Lastly, keep your mouth busy with sugar-free gum, hard candies, and lollipops.

Buff Away Nail Ridges and Surface Stains

Buffing can help smooth nail ridges, give nails a shinier appearance (even without polish), and increase circulation beneath the nails, which can help them grow. The key to buffing nails is to do it carefully and with a light hand so you don't damage or injure your nail (which can cause white spots or even more ridges). After removing any nail polish, provide a protective layer to cuticles by dabbing them with olive oil and to nails by applying a lightweight hand cream. For five to ten seconds, lightly buff each nail moving the buffer in one direction, not sawing back and forth. This evens out the nail's surface and makes it shiny, whereas buffing back and forth can thin and damage the nail and leave it susceptible to peeling. Choose a buffer that has a smooth, cushioned surface and doesn't feel like a nail file. Test it by rubbing it on your arm; if it feels too abrasive against your skin, it's not good for your nails. And never use an emery board since its rough surface is too harsh. In lieu of a buffer, you can also use a terrycloth washcloth.

Moisturize

Nails and cuticles need to be moisturized, since most problems crop up when they're dry. Dry nails can crack, peel, and get brittle. And, dehydrated cuticles can turn into painful and infected hangnails. The best moisturizers are thick—even greasy—but any good hand moisturizer will do.

Accelerate Growth

Everyone has an individual rate at which her nails increase in length. On average, nails gain about ⅛ inch per month. That growth can be influenced by hormonal changes (which is why pregnant women's nails grow like crazy) and temperature (more growth in summer than in winter). There's no single food or pill that will speed nail growth, and it's well-known that poor nutrition, infections, and aging can all slow it. To keep nails healthy, follow my seven-day plan. I also recommend a nail hardener like OPI Nail Envy to help prevent breakage.

Beware: Fungus

A fungal infection can settle in without you even realizing it. To be on the safe side, periodically remove any polish and inspect your fingers and toes. Fungus is contagious and can spread from one nail to another—and even from nails to skin. These infections aren't dangerous, but they can be painful and unsightly. What's more, fungal nail infections account for about 50 percent of all nail disorders, according to the American Academy of Dermatology.

If you see your nail thickening, yellowing, crumbling, or lifting from its bed (as if it's about to fall off), these are signs that a fungus might be settling in.

Because the infection occurs under the nail plate or in the nail bed, successful treatment may take several months or more. I suggest talking to your doctor about a prescription oral medication (like Lamisil). For new or mild cases, a topical medication may help.

To prevent fungus in the future, wash and dry your feet thoroughly. Keep your shoes on in public places. If your feet sweat a lot, change your socks often.

Strengthen with a supplement. Biotin is a B vitamin that is believed to strengthen nails (and hair), while being deficient in this nutrient can lead to weak, peeling, and dry nails. The recommended daily allowance is 300 micrograms.

Help Brittle Nails

If your nails are quick to peel, split, or chip, then you may have brittle nails like millions of other Americans. This happens when the hard part of the nail that is made of layers of dead cells gets dehydrated and less flexible. This condition can develop or get worse as you age, if you're frequently exposed to harsh chemicals (like cleaning products) or your hands are often submerged in water for long periods of time. Wear gloves when cleaning and putting hands in water and hydrate cuticles and nails nightly before bed. Also, when filing weak, brittle nails don't saw back and forth with your file, which can cause peeling and split-ting, but go in one direction.

Here's how to put all this advice into a plan that will transform your nails in just seven days.

 ## Day 1

All I want you to do today is head out to a good nail spa and have a manicure (no artificial nails!)—just a manicure that incorporates a moisturizing nail and cuticle treatment.

 ## Day 2

Apply my Citrus Cuticle Treatment.

Moisturize your nails with a product such as Elizabeth Arden Eight Hour Hand Cream.

Day 3

Moisturize your nails.

Apply a clear top coat to help preserve your polish, and make your manicure last longer.

Day 4

Apply my Citrus Cuticle Treatment.

Moisturize your nails.

Day 5

Remove your nail polish.

Buff your nails.

Moisturize your nails prior to bedtime.

Day 6

Here's an easy, at-home manicure to make nails look better and polish last longer.

Exfoliate bare nails with a mix of ¼ cup brown sugar, 1 teaspoon agave, and 1 teaspoon olive or vegetable oil (you can also use cuticle oil). Exfoliating creates a smoother surface for your polish so it goes on more easily and looks better. Lightly rub the brown sugar scrub on each nail for ten seconds, and then let it sit for one minute so the cuticles can soak in some of oil. Then rinse well with lukewarm water.

Cover one index finger with a soft washcloth, and use light pressure to gently push small sections of the cuticle back at a time.

Wash and dry hands completely to remove any oil residue, which will prevent polish from sticking as well, and go over each nail with a chemical-free nail polish remover.

File nails using a light touch and going in one direction; sawing back and forth can cause peeling, splitting and broken nails. Don't file the sides of the nails—this can weaken them—and don't file them into a point, or they'll break more easily.

If nails have ridges, use a product called a "ridge filler" before any other basecoat or polish. This fills in the ridges so polish looks smoother.

Help prevent breakage with a hardener like OPI Nail Envy.

When you polish nails, apply two coats. But the key is to let the first coat dry for about three to four minutes before applying the next so polish adheres better.

Seal the tips of the nail with a light swipe of polish across the tips. Let nails air dry for three minutes. Nail-drying machines can actually make polish dry with small air bubbles and unevenly.

Then put nails into a cup of ice water. This hardens the polish so chips and smudges are less likely.

Day 7

Wash your nails to remove dirt and oil. Apply a clear top coat to make polish last longer.

Moisturize your nails and cuticles.

 FACT OR FICTION?

Eating Jell-O will strengthen my nails.

Fiction. This rumor seems to have started way back when one brand of gelatin was trying to market itself. They said that gelatin contained protein, the same substance nails are made of. Jell-O is gelatin combined mostly with sugar, water, and food coloring and doesn't contain enough protein to make any difference.

➡ BEHIND THE SCIENCE

If you've been to the salon for a manicure, you're probably familiar with the nail dryers that emit UV light. They're a favorite of many women since they shorten the time they have to wait. But these dry nails with UV light of the same wavelength, emit the same amount of radiation, and use the same light bulbs as tanning beds, which are known to cause cancer. Though more research needs to be done to confirm this, it makes sense, so I suggest the fan-type nail dryers. It may take a bit longer, but they don't put you at risk of potential skin cancer on your nails, fingers, or hands.

ASK DR. O

Can I prevent peeling, breaking, and splitting?

Exposure to water is most often the culprit here. The more you soak, the drier your nails become, and they'll weaken over time. Detergents in soaps, household cleansers, and some nail polish removers can also damage nails. Wear rubber gloves during chores. After hand washing, apply a rich moisturizer to nails to replace the natural oils that water washes away. Using a polish (even clear) or a cuticle oil (like Creative Nail Design SolarOil) helps provide a protective shield.

SEE YOUR M.D. ASAP

Your nails can be windows into your health, so see your doctor if you experience any of the following.

- ▢ If your nails have normally been strong and now they're brittle, splitting, or weak, this may be a symptom of a fungus, psoriasis, or an underactive thyroid.

- While superficial, vertical ridges are a natural part of the aging process or the result of an injury to the nail, deep horizontal ridges may be a sign of Lyme disease, diabetes, kidney disease, liver problems, or circulation issues in the body.

- A dark spot that grows as your nail grows out is likely a bruise from banging or injuring your finger. But if the dark spot is near or on the cuticle or doesn't grow out as your nail does, it could be a sign of melanoma, the deadliest form of skin cancer.

➡ THE FINAL ANSWER ON...

Bringing your own tools to a salon manicure.

Patients ask me about this often, and I say that it is a must to prevent germs and bacteria. Either bring your own set each time or, if you're a regular, leave your manicure kit (which should include everything from files to nail clippers to cuticle nippers) at the salon. (The same goes for pedicure tools.) Even though some salons put their tools in sterilizing machines, you can't be sure that the tools are in there long enough to make a difference, and some tools like nail files can't be sterilized.

---

better feet in 7

I've met some of the most incredibly beautiful women in my time, and believe it or not, they often have rather revolting feet. In fact, the more beautiful the lady, the more likely she is to have corns and blisters. Why? Blame it on her love of skyscraper high heels.

Not that I have anything against high heels or any shoe for that matter, but sexy shoes call for sexy feet, and keeping them that way is easy if you have the right tools, information, and daily plan.

By that I don't mean plastic surgery treatments—and yes, those do exist. Women are paying thousands of dollars for foot face-lifts in which they have toe bones removed or their feet "sculpted." Pardon the pun, but I'm not pulling your leg or foot! Some have even asked for toe liposuction, all in the name of making their feet look daintier. Others want their feet shaped or toes shortened. It gets worse. Once someone asked me to amputate some of their toes because their feet were too wide for the trendiest shoe styles. Seriously!

I believe in and advise basic cosmetic care for feet. After all, every day our feet do the bump and grind inside our shoes, whether we're wearing Nikes or Prada heels. In fact, the average person takes 8,000 to 10,000 steps each day. This creates a lot of wear and tear on the feet. Because our feet don't produce any oil to prevent dry skin (just plenty of sweat to chafe and chap), keeping up appearances from the ankles down is rarely an effortless endeavor. But with a regular program of pampering, you can put some sexiness in your step. Here's my seven-day program.

Day 1

Toned ankles enhance a lovely pair of legs, plus keep puffiness in check. Do the following exercise three times every day. Simply point and flex each foot ten times.

Today, I want you to start the seven days with a professional spa pedicure. This will make you feel good about your feet.

Day 2

Following a shower or bath, massage a moisturizer onto your feet and toes. If your skin is very dry, try putting on socks afterward to help skin absorb the lotion.

Trim your toenails correctly. First, cut straight across, keeping the end of each nail shorter than the tip of your toe. Gently round off the corners with an emery board. This helps guard against ingrown toenails.

Wear clean socks. Change socks or hosiery every day, especially after a workout.

Wear shoes that fit. If they're too tight, extra sweat can cause skin and nail problems. Most of us tend to have one foot that is slightly larger than the other, so shop for shoes that fit the bigger one.

Wear shower shoes in public places such as gyms and pool locker rooms, which are germ havens.

Do my point-and-flex exercise three times today.

Day 3

Soak away the rough spots. Combine 1 cup grapefruit juice, 1 cup lime juice, and 1 cup lemon juice with 1 cup of water in a basin that's large enough for your feet. Then soak feet for 15 minutes. The natural alpha hydroxy fruit acids in these citrus juices will exfoliate dead cells and dry skin on soles, leaving feet smoother.

Scrub your feet even softer. After the citrus soak, the dead skin should be loose and easier to remove. Mix together ½ cup of uncooked rice (brown or white), 2 tablespoons of agave, and 2 teaspoons of fresh, grated ginger. Apply this scrub to damp feet making sure to rub it on rough areas for about two to three minutes. Rinse with lukewarm water, and pat dry with a towel. Alternatively, with a pumice stone, gently and gradually rub down rough patches, dead skin, and corns with a pumice stone or emery board.

Hydrate your feet while you sleep. Before bed, mix together ½ cup of mayonnaise and ½ cup of mashed avocado. Apply this to the entire foot (for larger feet you may need to double the recipe). Cover with plastic wrap and then slip on long socks that have been warmed in the dryer because the heat helps these hydrating ingredients penetrate skin better. You can also warm the socks using a hair dryer. After you slip them on, climb into bed. (You may want to sleep on old sheets the nights you do this.) In the morning, remove socks and wrap, rinse soles in the shower and feel how smooth and soft they are.

Do my point-and-flex exercise three times today.

Day 4

Wash and dry your feet after your morning shower or bath.

Apply a special foot balm cream to your feet.

Do my point-and-flex exercise three times today.

Day 5

Wash and dry your feet after your morning shower or bath.

Apply a special foot balm cream to your feet.

Do my point-and-flex exercise three times today.

 ## Day 6

Soak away the rough spots again today, using my citrus soak.

Scrub your feet even softer with ½ cup of uncooked rice (brown or white), 2 tablespoons of agave, and 2 teaspoons of fresh, grated ginger. Apply this scrub to damp feet making sure to rub it on rough areas for about two to three minutes. Rinse with lukewarm water, and pat dry with a towel.

Hydrate your feet while you sleep, as described earlier.

Day 7

Get into the habit of checking your toenails for fungus. Nail fungus in an infection in the living part of your nail, called the nail bed. It exists below the hard, dead surface that we call the *nail*. (The formal name for it is the *nail plate*.) Symptoms include a nail that's thickened, lifting off the nail bed, brittle, crumbly, distorted, dark, or yellow in color. It can also hurt and have a strong, not-so-pleasant odor. Because a nail fungal infection, which is called *onychomycosis*, is so hard to reach, it's not easy to get rid of and isn't one of those skin conditions that will go away on its own. A healthy nail needs to grow in order to totally get rid of the fungus, so how long it takes to do so varies from person to person. One treatment option is a topical antifungal medication. These are available in both over-the-counter and prescription versions. Because these are applied on top of the nail, it's unclear how well they can reach the infection that lies beneath it. Because of this, you may want to see your doctor for a prescription oral medication that seems to attack the fungus from within.

If you follow this seven-day program on a continuous basis, you'll not only have sexy feel, you'll have happy feet too.

ASK DR. O

How do I know what kind of arch I have, and why is this important?

The arch is the area of the foot that provides a lot of support to your body. So, you need to choose shoes that match the type of arch you have; otherwise, you increase your risk for back pain, knee problems, and foot issues like plantar fasciitis and tendinitis. Figuring out what kind of arch you have is simple. Fill a bucket of water, step your bare foot in the water until it's wet thoroughly. Step onto a piece of heavy paper and then take a look at your footprint. If you don't see a lot of your foot in the print, you have a high arch. If you see a print of your entire foot, you have a low arch. If you see a footprint that resembles what's typically drawn to represent a footprint with the ball of the foot and toes on top, a curved area, and then the heel, you have a normal arch.

 ASK DR. O

I love new shoes but not the blisters that come with them. What can I do to prevent them?

Blisters are caused by friction. Reduce this by applying petroleum jelly between your foot and shoe or find a foot product made just for this purpose. Blisters also arise when shoes are too big or too small or when feet sweat, so get shoes that fit, and wear socks and stockings made of materials that wick sweat away from feet.

➡ THE FINAL WORD ON...

Finding shoes that fit and don't hurt.

Fashion often trumps comfort when it comes to shoes. But wearing high heels or uncomfortable shoes over the long term can cause serious foot problems and pain. Emily Splichal is a podiatrist we've had on the show, and we talked about healthy shoes. Here are some of the things she suggests that you look for:

- ☐ Padding, especially in the heel and ball of the foot. This cushions the foot and acts as a shock absorber.
- ☐ Flexibility under the ball of the foot.
- ☐ Soles that absorb shock. Ideally, that would mean rubber.
- ☐ Stable heels. Stilettos are popular, but more substantial heels like wedges offer more support.
- ☐ A back. The back of the shoe provides more support to the foot.
- ☐ Natural materials help feet breathe so they don't sweat as much (which helps prevent blisters).

If the shoe fits, wear it. This may sound obvious, but plenty of people wear shoes that don't fit just because they like the style. Shop for shoes at the end of the day when your feet are the largest, and get measured each time you shop. Surprisingly, your shoe size can change as an adult from things like weight gain or loss, pregnancy, or the natural aging process.

 SEE YOUR M.D. ASAP

If you notice a dark spot on a toenail, see a dermatologist to rule out skin cancer. It could be a bruise from too-tight shoes or banging your toenail, and you'll know it's just a banged-up toe if the discoloration grows out as the nail grows. But don't wait for your nail to grow because catching cancer early is crucial. (In fact, reggae artist Bob Marley died because of a melanoma on his toe that he thought was a bruise from playing soccer.)

FACT OR FICTION?

Duct tape can get rid of a wart.

It's true that just one of duct tape's hundreds of uses is to get rid of warts. It's believed to work because chemicals in the tape actually stop the wart from growing and eventually kill it. To use this method, clean the wart and surrounding area gently. Next, apply a piece of duct tape that's just a bit larger than the wart. Press the duct tape to ensure that it adheres to the wart and surrounding skin. Remove and replace duct tape every three days until the wart is gone. Another unique remedy for removing warts, plantar warts, or just really rough calluses is to tape a small piece of banana peel over the area and replace daily until the skin is healed.

better sex in 7

Is doing it becoming a bore and a chore? Has the spark vanished from your sex life? Are you so wiped out by bedtime that getting it on seems like *Mission Impossible*?

A low sex drive is rampant these days, so much so that the prestigious *Journal of the American Medical Association* (JAMA) recently published the findings of a study on diminished libido. Disturbing news: More than 40 percent of American women can't do it or don't want to do it. Are you among them? If so, not to worry...here's where I show you how to turn from ice queen to sex fiend—in just seven days.

better libido in 7

First, why the dip in your desire? For many women, it has to do with fluctuating hormones due to menopause, mainly a drop in the hormones, progesterone, testosterone, and estrogen. Hormonal decline triggers a variety of disturbing symptoms, many of which affect your libido. Vaginal dryness is one of worst, because it makes sex hurt. (Lubrication with over-the-counter products can resolve this symptom very quickly.)

My first piece of advice is this: Please have more sex, starting now, whether you feel like it or not. Act as if you want it...then do it. There's a fundamental, physiological reason why: Sex causes your body to churn out more testosterone, a hormone that fuels desire. This is crucial, since after you hit 30, your testosterone levels fall. If you have an active partner, this is the most natural way to reclaim your sexual desire. Make dates for sex, if you have to. It may feel contrived at first, but as you carve out time for intimacy initially, it will get—and feel—more spontaneous.

I want you to have more sex not just because it's fun and pleasurable—not to mention that a healthy sex life promotes bonding, closeness, and trust—but because as a doctor, sex (safe sex, that is) is good for your health. In a 25-year study, scientists found that women who enjoyed sex lived longer than those with less positive experiences. Researchers can't explain why sex will make you live longer, but I have a theory. I think it's because vigorous sex can pump up the volume of oxygen taken into your lungs, accelerate your heart rate, and increase your blood circulation, all of which benefit your general health. Sex can also help you nip potentially dangerous habits in the bud. When you're sexually fulfilled, you feel better about yourself. You're less likely to abuse drugs, drink excess alcohol, or indulge in junk food. Finally, sex is a great remedy for stress. If you're feeling anxious or worried, if you need to get your mind off things and work off some tension, consider spending an evening in the sack with your beloved.

If your overall health is pretty good, there are some nutritional supplements that can restore your desire. Of course, the best place to begin is with a nutritious diet and regular exercise. Good nutrition is super important; it affects all the brain chemicals and hormones that play a role in sexuality. I recommend a well-balanced diet, with the focus on low-fat food. If you're trying to digest a lot of greasy foods, you probably won't have the get-up-and-go for sex.

Here are some specific natural products to try:

☐ **A complete multivitamin/mineral formula.** Take this daily to ensure good intake of nutrients needed for the production of sex hormones and energy.

☐ **ArginMax for Women.** This supplement contains the amino acid arginine, which works in way similar to what makes Viagra work. Arginine boosts the body's production of nitric oxide, which relaxes and dilates blood vessels, thereby promoting better blood flow to the genitals. This supplement also contains a blend of herbs, vitamins, and minerals. In a Stanford study of 77 women of all ages, 74 percent of those taking ArginMax for Women reported improved sexual satisfaction (desire, vaginal dryness, and sensation) compared to 37 percent in the placebo group. So, I'd say there's some validity to this supplement. But if you don't want to supplement, eat foods high in arginine, including nuts, seeds, whole grains, and chocolate.

☐ **Xzite.** This product is a mixture of Chinese herbs believed to increase blood flow to the genital area, boost muscle relaxation, and stimulate the mood center of the brain. The net effect is increased desire, lubrication, sensation, and ease of orgasm, supposedly after two weeks of consistent use. I don't see any harm in trying it, at least for two weeks, to see what happens to your sex drive.

☐ **Oriental ginseng (Panax ginseng).** This popular herb has been considered an aphrodisiac for thousands of years. In an Italian study, researchers noted that ginseng's ability to enhance physical performance also included sexual performance. Typically, doses start at 100 to 200 milligrams per day. Although the herb is widely considered to be safe, if you have high blood pressure, talk to your doctor before supplementing with it.

Now, if you want a better sex drive but aren't quite in the mood, follow my seven-day program, and your drive and desire should swing into explosively high gear each passing day.

Day 1

Take a multivitamin/multimineral with breakfast, plus one of the supplements recommended earlier (follow the manufacturer's directions for dosage).

Play the centerfold tonight. Toss your hair around, and give your best come-hither look. Then have your husband or boyfriend take smoldering pictures of you.

List ten things that make you feel sexy: Examples are wearing silky lingerie to bed, donning your favorite low-cut outfit, having a makeover, or being complimented by your hubby or romantic partner. Make a point of doing and experiencing these things more often. This exercise will help you feel hotter than ever.

▦ Day 2

Take a multivitamin/multimineral with breakfast, plus one of the supplements recommended earlier (follow the manufacturer's directions for dosage).

Commit to losing weight (try my "Thinner in 7" diet in Chapter 1). Being too heavy not only affects your sexual confidence but can also throw your hormones out of whack. Extra fat can manufacture excess estrogen. This can upset your hormonal balance, trigger mood swings, and lead to a low sex drive. Change your eating and exercise habits, and you'll correct these problems and restore your libido in no time. (See the "Aphrodisiac Foods" table for foods that really work.) Stick to a diet rich in lean proteins, whole grains, fruits, and vegetables; this can help increase the amount of blood circulation to your hoo-hoo, and with it, more lubrication, greater arousal, and more powerful orgasms. Start eating lean today.

APHRODISIAC FOODS

SEXY FOODS	HOW THEY WORK
Asparagus and Avocados	Both greens contain vitamin E, which helps your body produce testosterone, estrogen, and progesterone. All three hormones circulate in your bloodstream and stimulate sexual responses like clitoral swelling and vaginal lubrication.
Bananas	Yes, a banana is shaped like his penis, but the key benefit here is that bananas deliver potassium, a nutrient that helps maximize muscle strength. So when you orgasm, your contractions will be more intense.
Chocolate	Cocoa is loaded the chemical phenylethylamine, a stimulant that spurs sexual desire and excitement.
Hot Chilies	Capsaicin, a chemical found in hot peppers, boosts circulation. That gets blood pumping and stimulates nerve endings so you'll be more in the mood.
Oysters	Okay, oysters as an aphrodisiac sounds so clichéd, but they can really turn you on. These shellfish are packed with zinc, a mineral that cranks up the production of testosterone.
Pomegranates	This fruit owes its passion power to antioxidants, which protect the lining of blood vessels, allowing more blood to course through your genitals. The pom also helps increase vaginal lubrication.

SEXY FOODS	HOW THEY WORK
Red Wine	Red wine contains resveratrol, an antioxidant that helps boost blood flow to your nether regions.
Salmon and Walnuts	Both foods are brimming with omega-3 fatty acids, which keep sex-hormone production at its peak.
Vanilla	After a romantic candlelit dinner, lick an ice cream cone flavored with this sweet bean. It mildly stimulates nerves, heightening sexual arousal.
Watermelon	This juicy fruit contains the phytonutrient citrulline, which leads to a surge of nitric oxide in your body. That spike causes blood vessels to relax and speeds up circulation. Again, the more blood flow, the greater your arousal.

Move your body. Physical activity amps up your libido because it helps lift and sustain energy levels. Exercise also pumps more blood your genitals, increasing your capacity for sexual arousal. A calming activity like yoga helps soothe the mind and body when stress contributes to your flagging sex drive. Commit to exercising every day. Schedule exercise on your calendar, even if it's a 30-minute walk around your neighborhood.

Have sex or masturbate.

 # Day 3

Take a multivitamin/multimineral with breakfast, plus one of the supplements recommended earlier (follow the manufacturer's directions for dosage).

Write down your food plan for the day (see my "Slimmer in 7" diet for rapid weight loss). Then follow your plan to the letter.

Make time to exercise. Do a home workout DVD like Pilates or yoga, but do it naked. Working out in the buff helps you experience your sensuality.

Have sex or masturbate.

Day 4

Take a multivitamin/multimineral with breakfast, plus one of the supplements recommended earlier (follow the manufacturer's directions for dosage).

Write down your food plan for the day (see my "Slimmer in 7" diet for rapid weight loss). Then follow your plan to the letter.

Make time to exercise.

Make love in unexpected places today, anywhere except your bedroom. Even just doing it in the living room seems like an adventure sometimes. I also like the idea of a weekend getaway—maybe just a night?—so you can get back to who you are together.

Day 5

Take a multivitamin/multimineral with breakfast, plus one of the supplements recommended earlier (follow the manufacturer's directions for dosage).

Write down your food plan for the day (see my "Slimmer in 7" diet for rapid weight loss). Then follow your plan to the letter.

Make time to exercise.

Zap stress, tension, anxiety, and depression; these are all enemies of sexual arousal. Bear in mind that stress will weaken you physically and block the biochemical action needed to heighten sex drive. Quick fix suggestion: Schedule a massage. A good rubdown not only helps you reconnect with your body and build sexual awareness but can also help extinguish tension that might be interfering with your ability to relax and get in the mood. One massage session may do the trick; however, regular massages can help maintain a sense of sexual well-being and appreciation for your sensuality.

Have sex tonight with your hubby or partner.

Day 6

Take a multivitamin/multimineral with breakfast, plus one of the supplements recommended earlier (follow the manufacturer's directions for dosage).

Write down your food plan for the day (see my "Slimmer in 7" diet for rapid weight loss). Then follow your plan to the letter.

Make time to exercise.

Get into sexting to set the mood. *Sexting* is sending sexy, suggestive messages, or photos to your partner. Example: "I'm looking forward to kissing you everywhere." This communication builds sexual tension and desire for later. That said, there are some rules of sext etiquette to follow: Don't send anything you don't want the world to see, make sure the sext goes to the intended person, and don't do any sexting on your company-issued cell phone. And by the way, don't spend too much time doing it either. Regularly squinting to read your phone's small text strains the muscles between and around your eyes.

Take a bath with your spouse or partner. Use a jasmine-scented bath oil, known to boost sexual desire.

Day 7

Take a multivitamin/multimineral with breakfast, plus one of the supplements recommended earlier (follow the manufacturer's directions for dosage).

Write down your food plan for the day (see my "Slimmer in 7" diet for rapid weight loss). Then follow your plan to the letter.

Make time to exercise.

Exfoliate your entire body today to make your skin smooth and sensual for sex. Use my full-body scrub below.

Watch a scary flick with your partner. This may seem strange, but an underestimated aphrodisiac is fear. It can spark sexual desire.

Have sex or masturbate.

Now if this seven-day program is working for you, let's take it to the next level—better orgasms in seven days. Turn the page to find out how.

✚ DR. ORDON'S FULL BODY SCRUB

Mix together:

- ¼ cup brown sugar
- ¼ cup Kosher salt
- ¼ cup olive oil or coconut oil
- ½ teaspoon cinnamon.

Rub it all over your body to exfoliate your skin. Wash off.

📋 SEE YOUR M.D. ASAP

If you have a low sex drive, talk to your doc. It can be caused by any number of physical conditions: diabetes, heart disease, thyroid disease, anemia, childbirth, menopause, hysterectomy, and medical problems that affect sex hormones. Other causes include stress, depression, anxiety, other emotional problems, or any combination of these factors. Your physician may want to check you for any medical and psychological issues like these that affect sex drive.

better orgasms in 7

Let me state unequivocally, without blushing or embarrassment: Every woman is capable of having an orgasm. Yet approximately 10 percent of women never have one, and a lot of women don't experience one during intercourse. Let's change that, because having earth-moving orgasms, and lots of them, is really not that difficult. It is one of those incredible joys of life that is free.

Inability to climax during intercourse is the second most common sexual complaint I hear from women, behind lack of sexual desire. If you're not having orgasms, then I'm willing to bet you don't want to have sex that often, which creates a whole catalog of relationship problems.

What exactly is an orgasm? An orgasm usually comes from your clitoris, an area with thousands of nerve endings just above the urethra (where the urine comes out). Only the tip is visible; the rest of the clitoris lies under the labia (the lips of your vagina).

The pelvic floor muscles are also involved in orgasm. These muscles include the bulbospongiosus muscle, the perineal muscles, and the pubococcygeus muscle. They extend from above the clitoris down past and around the entrance to the vagina. Using these muscles during sex can be pleasurable and also help with having an orgasm.

When you're turned on, blood flow to your vagina increases, lubricating and swelling the inner and outer lips and the clitoris. During this period of arousal, intense stimulation—both physical and psychological—leads to orgasm, during which the vagina, anal sphincter, and uterus contract in simultaneous spasms.

I'm frequently asked about an area of the female anatomy that gets a lot of press for supposedly being an erotic epicenter: the "G-spot," named after Ernest Grafenberg, the German doctor who "discovered" it in the 50s. The G-spot is a rough patch of skin located on the upper vaginal wall. To locate it, insert your ring finger in your vagina and make a beckoning gesture forward, with the finger against the rear vaginal wall. The rough place is your G-spot. If you enjoy having it stroked, great. If not, forget it.

Back to the clitoris for a moment. It's what really packs the pleasure punch—let's call it the C-spot. There are more nerve endings in the C-spot than there are inside the vagina. Interestingly, the only purpose of the clitoris is to bring you to orgasm. It has no other function! So, it's rare to have an orgasm without some sort of clitoral stimulation.

Okay, let's dispense with Orgasm 101 and do some homework, before I give you my seven-day program.

Pleasure Principle #1

Learn to masturbate. Masturbation is important—for two reasons. You discover what you need to reach orgasm. You get your body into the groove of having orgasms regularly. This is the starting point on your path to mind-blowing orgasms—and plenty of them.

Women who love sex are okay with masturbation, and they do it frequently. It's how you can learn about your body, about what you like, and about how you can reach orgasm quickly or slowly.

Pleasure Principle #2

Do Kegels. These are strength training for your pubococcygeus (PC) muscles—the ones that support your vagina, anus, uterus, bladder, and urethra. Just like your biceps or hamstrings, these muscles remade of slow- and fast-twitch fibers. Together, they account for sheer power and allow your vagina to "grab." On their own, fast-twitch fibers also produce and sustain the feeling of orgasm. I prescribe a 10-second hold, followed by a 10-second rest, repeated 60 times over 20 minutes. It should be done at least twice a day for seven days, continuing for 5 to 7 more weeks, with biweekly maintenance thereafter. It makes a difference. The stronger these muscles are, the more intense your orgasms will be, I promise.

Don't know how to work out your Kegels? Next time you urinate, try stopping the flow. The muscles you use are your Kegel muscles. Just don't make it a habit to do Kegels when you urinate; stopping and starting the flow continuously can increase your risk for urinary tract infections.

Pleasure Principle #3

Pump up your exercise program. Fit women have better orgasms—and more of them. Two of the best exercises for sexual fitness are swimming and Pilates. Not only will swimming give you a body to die for, it will also boost your libido and performance too. It's one of the best exercises for your sex life because it tones your pelvic floor muscles. Translation: better orgasms for you. Swimming also increases stamina, essential for marathon sex sessions, and improves a flagging sex drive because it makes you feel more relaxed than other exercise.

Doing regular Pilates classes can also help you have better orgasms. Pilates strengthens the muscles of the lower abdomen and tightens pelvic floor muscles. Increased pelvic and hip flexibility also make it easier to try to hold new sexual positions without getting cramps in your legs and thighs.

Pleasure Principle #4

Staying lubricated is crucial to achieving an orgasm. Try lubrication products like Vibrance Cream, Zestra Feminine Arousal Fluid, or KY Jelly.

Red flag warning: Some personal lubricants contain chemicals and preservatives that can irritate your tissues. Not only that, research has found that some brands essentially kill sperm viability, with zero motility after 30 minutes of exposure, and may damage rectal and vaginal tissue.

📋 NATURAL LUBRICATION TIPS

- ☐ **Stay hydrated.** Drinking plenty of water through the day helps treat the dryness in your vagina, plus confers many other health benefits of staying hydrated.

- ☐ **Quit smoking.** There are hundreds of reasons to quit, but know that cigarette smoking depletes estrogen, which helps your vagina stay lubricated.

- ☐ **Supplement with anti-dryness herbs.** Holistic health care practitioners recommend dong quai, fennel, fenugreek, chasteberry, or black cohosh to aid lubrication. If you decide to supplement, read the label for dosage instructions and talk to your physician about supplementing.

- ☐ **Eat foods high in phytoestrogens.** These include soy, apples, nuts, flaxseed, celery, alfalfa, and whole grains. Phytoestrogens naturally mimic estrogen in your body. See my recipe Dr. Ordon's Orgasmic Smoothie.

- ☐ **Talk to your doctor about using a prescription vaginal cream.** These medicines are particularly helpful if you're postmenopausal.

- ☐ **Do it more often.** Regular sexual activity and stimulation will increase the blood flow to the area, which will help boost your natural lubrication.

Pleasure Principle #5

Position yourself. The most orgasmic sex position for women is usually on top. You-on-top is great because you're in control and have choices: You can grind yourself against his pubic bone for stimulation, you can stimulate yourself, or you can guide his hand to stimulate you. You can also control the penetration to a depth that feels best.

Pleasure Principle #6

Think your way to an orgasm. This is entirely possible because your body can respond to thoughts the same way it responds to physical touch. Sexy thoughts trigger the sexual center of the brain—a complex system that includes the hypothalamus, which kicks your body's arousal cycle into high gear. Start meditating on racy thoughts, or focus on relaxing imagery like walking on the beach. Be aware of every feeling you have as you let your arousal build. If this doesn't lead to orgasm right away, try thinking sensual thoughts before bed. Your brain can do very surprising things if you meditate in this manner.

Pleasure Principle #7

Soak up some rays. Sunshine will make you feel like having sex more often (and more sex can lead to more orgasms). Why? Because sunlight boosts testosterone not only in men but in women, too, and this hormone controls desire. It also ramps up the production of serotonin, the feel-good brain hormone.

There's more: High temps increase your blood circulation, and that means not only will you want more sex, you'll feel more responsive and may experience more intense orgasms. Go grab your sunglasses and some sunscreen...you're going to start feeling it!

- ☐ 1 cup unsweetened soy milk*
- ☐ 1 tablespoon ground flaxseeds
- ☐ ½ cup unsweetened applesauce
- ☐ 1 tablespoon honey
- ☐ 3 ice cubes

Blend together until smooth. Makes one serving.

*If you are allergic to soy milk, substitute almond or rice milk.

Now for my seven-day program for better orgasms.

Day 1

Begin the day with my Orgasmic Smoothie for breakfast.

Get more aware of what brings you sensual and sexual pleasure. Write down what you enjoy. Examples: my nipples caressed; my butt stroked; my neck and/or thighs kissed...write it all down.

Practice your Kegel exercises.

Do Pilates or go for a swim.

Take a hot bath or shower in the evening. Remember, warm water relaxes you. Touch yourself. See what feels good. Try this for 10 to 15 minutes, and do it a few times a week.

Think your way to an orgasm by meditating on sensual thoughts that arouse you. If you do this prior to going to sleep, you may climax in your sleep—a phenomenon known as a "noctural orgasm."

Day 2

Begin the day with my Orgasmic Smoothie for breakfast.

Once you've figured out what works for you, clue your partner in, too. Trust me; he wants to know. Every one responds differently to sexual techniques, so communicate what works for you.

Practice masturbating.

Practice your Kegel exercises.

Have sex with your lover tonight. Be relaxed; don't overfocus on having an orgasm...simply enjoy the experience. Another tip: Try drinking 8 ounces of natural juice like orange juice or a sugary mug of hot chocolate prior to going to bed. Some extra sugar in your system energizes your libido and helps your body reach orgasm faster.

 ## Day 3

Begin the day with my Orgasmic Smoothie for breakfast.

Examine your self-talk. If you have a negative tape loop running through your thoughts ("my thighs are too fat...my tummy is too flabby"), hit the stop button! Negative internal dialogue squelches passion faster than you can say "orgasm." Trust me, again: If a guy is in bed with you, he's not thinking about whether your belly jiggles or your thighs have cellulite.

Practice your Kegel exercises.

Do Pilates or go for a swim.

Practice masturbating.

Have sex with your lover tonight. Remember, stay relaxed and enjoy the experience, whatever it brings.

 ## Day 4

Begin the day with my Orgasmic Smoothie for breakfast.

Practice masturbating.

Practice your Kegel exercises.

Think your way to an orgasm. Spend time meditating on sensual thoughts.

Have sex with your lover tonight. Be relaxed; don't overfocus on having an orgasm...simply enjoy the experience.

 ## Day 5

Begin the day with my Orgasmic Smoothie for breakfast.

Practice masturbating.

Practice your Kegel exercises.

Exercise today.

Work on your self-talk.

Have sex with your lover tonight. Be relaxed; don't overfocus on having an orgasm...simply enjoy the experience.

Day 6

Begin the day with my Orgasmic Smoothie for breakfast.

Practice masturbating.

Practice your Kegel exercises.

Ask your partner to play with your breasts during lovemaking. Intense breast stimulation makes your body release oxytocin, the chemical that makes you feel love and attachment. Oxytocin affects specific nerves that, with increasing levels of arousal, lead to orgasm.

Day 7

Begin the day with my Orgasmic Smoothie for breakfast.

Practice masturbating.

Practice your Kegel exercises.

Encourage your lover to stimulate you in the same way as you're able to stimulate yourself.

Change the pacing during intercourse, as well.

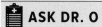 **ASK DR. O**

Does better foreplay lead to better orgasms?

NO. Longer sex does! A recent study found the ability to climax depended not on foreplay but on the "quality and duration" of sex. European scientists asked 2,360 women to track whether they had orgasms, and how long they'd engaged in foreplay and actual sex, whenever they got it on. The findings? Length of intercourse was more important for orgasms than foreplay. Focusing on vaginal sensations during intercourse—not before—is the orgasmic secret.

All orgasms are great. Thinking of them as brilliant or so-so just puts pressure on you. The trick is not to strive for something better; we all feel orgasms in different ways. My advice is to enjoy whatever happens.

better mind-body strategies in 7

So many things can get out of whack other than just your skin, figure, sex life, and general appearance. Sometimes you can just lose your ability to think normally, feel good, or have the energy to follow through on what you need to do to get better in seven days.

In this final part of the book, you'll be surprised and delighted to discover that a lot of what goes wrong in these areas is eminently preventable, mostly by adopting a few more, extra-easy lifestyle habits. So, if you want to become truly beautiful and sexier, inside and out, start by getting to know how to improve your sleep, mood, and energy levels.

better sleep in 7

Want to know one of the best and most trusted beauty tips? Getting enough sleep. Ignore sleep, and watch your complexion, your hair, and general well-being all go to hell. A lack of shut-eye can leave you with blah skin, puffy eyes, and a headache the size of Alaska.

I know what it's like to not be able to get a great night's sleep. Something that frequently happens to me—and makes me mad—is when I wake up at 3 or 4 a.m. and start tossing, turning, and worrying. Every 10 minutes I'll look at the lighted hands of the clock on the table next to my bed. I'm sure I haven't slept a wink since 3 a.m., and then, suddenly, at 5:30, my clock radio goes off—and wakes me. If the radio hadn't come on, I'd have sworn I never slept.

One night when I couldn't sleep, I turned on the light, made a cup of coffee, and sat in front of the TV, watching an infomercial for an ab-fat zapper.

The next thing I knew I was being attacked by my teenagers demanding breakfast, and I felt I had gone through three rounds with Mike Tyson.

As I sat there grumbling about how kids should learn to make coffee for their fathers by their teen years, one of my kids asked me why I was up so early.

Suddenly I felt really guilty. I spend hours with patients who can't sleep, talking to them about ways to improve their sleep, and here was I, doing the opposite of everything I tell them to do. So, to ease my conscience, I decided I would include a chapter in this book about sleep. Maybe then we can all get a better night's rest, myself included.

For starters, we spend about 24 years of our lives in bed; therefore, sleep is obviously important to our well-being. Scientists who study sleep claim that the most important aspect of a good night's rest is the amount of time you spend dreaming. They divide sleep into two distinct types, nonrapid eye movement (non-REM) and rapid eye movement (REM), or dream sleep. Non-REM has three phases.

Phase 1 is commonly called "dropping off." Here the brain begins to slow down its activity, sounds become more distant, and muscles begin to relax. The mind begins to wander around vague images of the day, and slowly after about 15 minutes the brain moves into phase 2, or intermediate sleep. This lasts about 20 minutes, during which time the body's temperature, heart rate, and blood pressure become stable.

As brain activity continues to slow down, the body moves into phase 3, or deep sleep. Now, breathing has slowed right down, there are no dreams, and the person is very difficult to rouse. In total, this whole process takes about an hour to an hour and a half.

From deep sleep, the brain then suddenly shifts into REM sleep. REM sleep helps the body and the immune system recharge and repair cell damage from the day's activities.

The body goes into a paralyzed-like state, except for the occasional muscle twitch; the eyes begin to quickly move backward and forward behind the eyelids, and the person begins to dream.

Dream sleep lasts only about 10 to 15 minutes before the whole cycle repeats itself, and the brain moves back to Phase 1 of non-REM. On average, this pattern repeats itself four times each night.

The total amount of dream sleep we need decreases with age. Babies spend 50 percent of their sleep dreaming, while by the time you are 80, only 10 percent of your sleep is taken up with dreams. As a result of this, we need less and less total sleep the older we get. A good way to look at it is that we lose an hour a decade, which is why elderly people sleep a lot less than their teenage grandchildren.

Amounts also vary from person to person. Some people seem to need a lot less sleep than others, though the average is 7 to 8 hours a night. People with certain sleep disorders need up to 17 hours a day, dreaming very little.

Sleep problems are very common, affecting more than half of us at some point in our lives. They can range from short-term insomnia due to jet lag to chronic disorders that last for years. Thankfully, most problems fix themselves, but sometimes a little medical help is needed.

Sleeping pills were at one point the most frequently prescribed drugs on the market and seemed to be the miracle cure. Soon, however, both doctors and patients noticed that not only were they addictive but they also seemed to make the problem worse in the long term. The main reason for this was the older sleeping pills stopped patients from going into REM sleep. So, when patients stopped taking them, the brain had to catch up on all the REM it had missed, resulting in very long and vivid dreams, which usually took the form of nightmares.

As you can imagine, having nightmares for weeks on end doesn't appeal to most people, so they would return to their doctor and be put back on the pills and start the whole process over again.

The best way to get a good night's sleep is to do it naturally. The first thing to remember is that the body needs sleep in the same way that a car needs gasoline, and it will get it, no matter what. What most people complain about, though, is not getting enough hours of uninterrupted sleep at night, so here are some general guidelines to help you:

◻ **Don't catnap during the day.** If you sleep even for 20 to 30 minutes during the day, your brain quickly goes into REM sleep, and you cut down the amount you need at night. This can be enough to stop one of the cycles mentioned earlier and can mean you lose up to 90 minutes of time asleep in bed.

◻ **Go to bed only when you're tired.** Having a regular "lights off" is good for children but not for adults with sleeping difficulties. Wait until you are nearly dropping off before you crawl through to the bedroom.

- ☐ **Get up at the same time every day.** Even if you get only two hours sleep, set your alarm to wake you at the same time (including weekends).

- ☐ **No caffeine after 6 p.m.** This includes tea, coffee, and most fizzy drinks. Caffeine is a powerful stimulant and can stay in your system for eight hours, which means a cup of tea at 9 p.m. is still keeping you awake at 5 a.m.

- ☐ **Always sleep in a dark room.** Switching the light on, even to go to the toilet, stimulates the brain to produce a hormone called *melatonin*, which tricks you into thinking it's daytime, and you wake up.

- ☐ **Your bed is for sleeping in.** People who sit on their beds to study, play computer games, or write letters get used to bed being a place for being awake.

Keep all of these pointers in mind. Now let's get a little more specific with my seven-day plan.

Day 1

Get in bed and read a boring book. If you do go to bed when you are not about to collapse, reading a dull book makes you lose concentration and increases your chances of drifting off.

Put your alarm clock where you can't see it. Most people who see every hour on the clock only do so because they look at the clock, so don't look.

As you begin to drift off, remember the old wives' tale: counting sheep actually does work.

Day 2

Try staying up a little later than usual every night. Okay, I don't want to offend everyone who goes to bed at 9 o'clock after a nice glass of warm milk, but generally speaking, people who go to bed late are more interesting than those who go to bed by 9. People who go to bed late enjoy life more and want to stay up as late as they can in order to live more of it. So, try hooting with the night owls once in a while!

🗓 Day 3

Go out today and shop for new pillows. Choose the right pillow to match your sleep style. There are pillows made to fit side sleepers, back sleepers, or stomach sleepers, and the right pillow can make a world of difference in giving you a satisfying and full night's rest.

Here are some other suggestions:

☐ Satin pillowcases relieve pressure on the bones and skin on your face, and this helps reduce the amount of skin wrinkling you'll get over time. Plus, the satin keeps your hair from getting mussed; you won't wake up with crazy-looking hair. And there's another bonus: softer skin. If you moisturize your skin nightly, a satin pillowcase won't absorb the lotion, so it's likelier to stay on your face.

☐ Got a partner who snores like a freight train? The Snore-No-More pillow helps position the head and chin for easier, snore-free snoozing.

☐ Use a firm, elevated pillow if you sleep on your back. This prevents body fluids from pooling into your facial tissues at night. In the morning, you'll awaken without puffy, baggy eyes.

🗓 Day 4

In addition to the previous suggestions, remember to use your night creams. They repair, refresh, and rejuvenate what was damaged during the day's exposure to sun, environmental factors, and simple stress. They can help improve skin tone and color, reduce blemishes, and hydrate and rejuvenate your skin.

Evening, before retiring, is a great time to practice a skin-care regimen, because in the quiet of your bedroom, you are free from stress, sun, and environmental factors that can cause premature aging. Giving yourself an "overnight facial" like this is a great way to wake up feeling refreshed and looking younger.

Day 5

Body temperature is important when you sleep. Sleep in a slightly cool room because this temperature mimics your internal temperature drop during sleep. If you feel cold, use blankets and wear socks. Research shows that warm hands and feet will help you fall asleep more quickly.

Select the right bedding. When selecting down, premium-quality larger-down clusters provide a higher fill power for lighter, softer loft and warmth in a comforter. Consider the construction of the comforter type of fabric and the thread count (the higher the thread count, the better).

Have any allergies? They can keep you awake at night. The proper hypoallergenic bedding will help lessen the possibility of an allergic reaction or response.

Don't exercise too close to bedtime. While exercise is a proven sleep aid, you shouldn't work out close to bedtime because, like caffeine, exercise has an alert effect. Give your body about three or four hours to rest down before you go to sleep.

Drink fewer fluids before you go to sleep. The more fluids you drink, the greater chances that you will wake up repeatedly for trips to the bathroom. Also, avoid heavy meals close to bedtime. If you must eat, do a light dinner about two hours before sleeping.

Day 6

Try some sweet-dream scents. Many perfumers believe that certain scents can help you (and your body) relax, making it easier to drift off to sleep. Some scents to try:

- **Lavender.** This floral scent is a true sleep aid. Moreover, a study conducted by the Smell & Taste Research Foundation in Chicago showed that lavender oil induces relaxation. (Another recommendation: Draw a scented bath with lavender oil, salts, or bubble bath.)

- **Chamomile.** The scent of chamomile has been used as a remedy for insomnia. It may also ease arthritis, which, according to the

National Sleep Foundation, disturbs the sleep of most people who have it. Have a cup of chamomile before hitting the sack.

□ **Linden blossom.** Often used as a relaxation ingredient in herbal teas, this scent can also be found in fragrances. (My recommendation: Before bed, massage linden blossom oil onto your shoulders and neck.)

Try a slumber-inducing snack. For example, increase your intake of tryptophan (through food, not supplements). This essential amino acid increases serotonin, a natural brain chemical that helps you relax and sleep. Include foods high in tryptophan with your dinner: three ounces of fish or poultry or a glass of milk. Even a few scoops of ice cream will help (if you're not on a diet!).

Also, use carbs to calm down. Foods high in carbohydrates also increase serotonin production. As a light evening snack, try a serotonin double-whammy of yogurt with fruit or the bedtime classic: cookies and milk.

Day 7

Take a bubble bath. And it needs to be a true bubble bath, because the bubbles provide insulation that keeps the water hotter. Baths don't just relax your muscles. It raises your core temperature. Then when you get out, your temperature drops, which helps your body manufacture melatonin, which helps you sleep.

Music helps you sleep better. If you're still having trouble sleeping, try listening to some classical music prior to tucking in. When 25 elderly patients with sleep problems listened to classical music right before bedtime, all but one reported improved sleep during the night, according to a study published in the *Journal of Holistic Nursing*. Improved sleep helps ward off numerous mind-numbing problems, such as lack of alertness, depression, and stress, to name just a few.

At night, while trying to fall asleep, if your mind goes into a spin cycle of thinking, take some deep breaths. I recommend a four-eight breath: Place the tip of your tongue against the ridge behind your upper front teeth. Breathe in through your nose to the count of four. Then, to the count of eight, breathe out through your mouth. Repeat several times.

Don't rely on meds. Of course, there will be nights when you want to just pop a pill. Pharmaceuticals such as Ambien and Restoril can be useful, but only in the short term.

Looking your best is as simple as getting a good night's rest. You deserve to look and feel beautiful, so try to get the amount of beauty sleep you deserve.

better mood in 7

A bad mood. Who needs it? Not you!

Without question, there's no bigger roadblock to a happy, sexy, productive life than a down-and-out mood. But here's some uplifting news: you can banish the blues—and do it in just seven days.

Did you know, for example, that there are blues-busting foods that are probably sitting in your kitchen or refrigerator right now? Or that there are some herbs and other supplements that offer astonishing protection against bad moods? Did you also know that optimism—one of the big secrets behind brain fitness, happiness, and longevity—can be learned and applied to your life?

Here is your personal seven-day plan to the answers you're seeking so that you can live life more fully, with an upbeat attitude and positive outlook toward the world around you.

📅 Day 1

Go to the grocery store and purchase the following good-mood foods. Try to eat at least three of them every day:

- ☐ **Brazil nuts:** They contain the mineral selenium, which has the ability to boost mood.
- ☐ **Calcium-containing foods, such as dairy products or leafy greens:** Calcium is calming, especially during episodes of premenstrual syndrome (PMS).
- ☐ **Fish:** Eating fish two to three times a week reduces symptoms of depression. One of the main reasons is that the good fats in fish increase the feel-good brain chemical serotonin.
- ☐ **Turkey breast:** Gobblers are full of an amino acid called *tyrosine*. Tyrosine is a precursor, or building block, to the brain chemicals dopamine and norepinephrine, both involved in helping the body better cope with stress.
- ☐ **Beef:** Red meat is the highest source of iron on the planet, and iron prevents fatigue-related blue moods. Eat two to three servings of lean red meat a week.
- ☐ **Whole-grain bread:** The benefit of this bread is in its mixture of brain-pleasing nutrients, named carbohydrates and amino acids, a combo that allows the most efficient delivery of tryptophan into the brain. Tryptophan is an amino acid that helps manufacture serotonin.
- ☐ **Spinach:** Popeye downed spinach for strength; now you can eat it for a mood boost. Spinach is high in folic acid, which eases depression.

Other mood-boosting foods to consider are bananas, oranges, jalapenos, and honey.

📅 Day 2

Head to the health food store today—not to the pharmacy—to stock up on a few natural tranquilizers to boost your mood. A caveat: Certainly, people who are seriously ill with clinical anxiety or depression need medication and should be under the care of a psychiatrist.

But for natural products, consider taking one of the following daily:

- **Chamomile:** It has a mild sedative effect; it contains active compounds known an angelic acid and apigenin. As a sedative or tranquilizer, take up to a gram of the powdered herb daily. If using a tincture, take 40 to 60 drops, mixed in juice or water, three to four times a day. Or you can consume the tea liberally, without any side effects.

- **Passionflower:** This herb exerts a gentle sedative action and has been found in studies to relieve anxiety, counter insomnia, and reduce high blood pressure. The normal dosage is 6 grams daily.

- **Valerian:** Hundreds of scientific studies have been conducted on this herb. Overall, the results have shown that the herb has a gentle tranquilizing effect. Herbalists suggest the following usage: capsules or tablets, 50 to 100 milligrams, taken two to three times a day to relieve stress.

Day 3

Here I go again: Please exercise daily, starting today. The more you make exercise a habit, the better your mood. But you have to make a true long-term commitment to it. Researchers in Australia studied three groups of people: long-term exercisers, short-term exercisers, and nonexercisers. The long-term group had a more positive outlook on life and were less depressed and stressed out than those in the other two groups.

So, in addition to eating mood-boosting foods and natural mood boosters, start moving today.

Day 4

See the light. If you want to keep a sunny disposition, get outdoors today and most days of the week as much as you can. Brighten up your house in the winter with more light or light coats of paint. Sit near windows. Exposure to sunlight increases levels of serotonin in your brain.

🗓 Day 5

Challenge your thinking today. Doctors know that most depression is caused by the way we respond to events and experiences. For example, some people take things personally, even when the situation is not personal. Or they look at life in terms of black and white, with no shades of gray. With either response, there can be a negative interpretation that can bring on depression.

In addition, try not to engage in all-or-nothing thinking. When faced with a situation, realize that there may be a variety of choices, rather than a single right choice you must make. Life can be ambiguous at times, with many possible paths to follow.

Take my test today to see whether you're a negative or positive thinker. Answer each question truthfully. At the end of the quiz, you'll be told whether you have a positive or negative explanatory style. Have fun!

➡ ARE YOU A NEGATIVE OR POSITIVE THINKER?

1. Your child is voted Most Valuable Player. You think:

   a. My child is a really good athlete.

   b. My child really lucked out.

2. You get hired for a job, even though there was some stiff competition. You think:

   a. I must be more qualified than I give myself credit for.

   b. I just gave a good interview.

3. You've planned a pool party, but it rains on that day. You think:

   a. Too bad. I'll just change everything so that the fun happens indoors.

   b. I should have planned better. I'm not really good with parties.

4. You're trying to figure out a new computer finance/money program, and after hours of work, you still can't understand it. You think:

   a. I'll keep at it. It will just take me a little longer to finally get this.

   b. I'm just not computer-literate.

5. You miss a flight and have to wait for another one. You think:

   a. If only there wasn't so much traffic! At least I'll make the next flight.

   b. I'm always late, and I knew this would happen.

6. You meet an important business contact at a networking event. You think:

   a. I was smart to attend this event tonight.

   b. I guess I was in the right place at the right time.

7. Someone cuts you off in traffic. You think:

   a. That person must be having a bad day.

   b. People are so rude!

8. You find you are in so much debt that it's hard to pay all your bills at the end of the month. You think:

   a. Oh, things will get better next month. It's just been a slow month for business.

   b. This is a serious problem. I need to get credit counseling and learn how to manage my money better.

9. You've been working hard at dieting, and you lose 10 pounds. You think:

   a. My effort is paying off. I'll be at my goal weight soon.

   b. This diet really works. I hope it helps me lose more.

10. You start a new workout program, and your muscles are really sore the next day. You think:

    a. I worked out hard yesterday.

    b. Boy, am I out of shape!

11. You get a speeding ticket, and you left your wallet and driver's license at home. You think:

    a. This just isn't my day!

    b. I'm such an idiot.

12. You win at bridge or some other card game. You think:

    a. I'm smart.

    b. I was just lucky.

13. You spot a dollar on the street. You think:

    a. I am very observant.

    b. Cool, I'm pretty lucky.

14. A co-worker compliments your new suit. You think:

    a. I must have a great sense of fashion.

    b. She's just trying to be nice.

15. You win a trivia contest. You think:

    a. I have a pretty good memory.

    b. I was lucky; the questions were easy.

Scoring: If most of your answers were *a*'s—eight or more—then you're a positive, realistic thinker. On the other hand, if most of your answers were *b*'s, you tend toward negative, somewhat pessimistic thinking.

Everyone has setbacks, even positive thinkers. A major difference between negative thinkers and positive thinkers, however, is how they respond to those setbacks. In the case of finding the dollar on the street, for instance, the answer that "I'm observant" shows that the positive event is because of an enduring and personal trait (being observant) rather than to a temporary external factor like luck.

Negative thinker tend to catastrophize situations, turning the proverbial molehill into a mountain. Or they worry over situations over which they have no control. Both approaches to life are paralyzing and unhealthy. They make things worse than they really are.

The next time you find yourself stuck in this kind of thinking, ask yourself these questions: What is the worst thing that can happen? How likely is that to occur? How much difference will this situation make in my life a year from now? Am I likely to remember it? This type of self-talk puts a more positive spin on the situation and keeps bad moods on check.

Day 6

Tonight, liven up your lovemaking (review Part 4). Intimate, fulfilling sex with a committed partner releases endorphins to produce a natural euphoria and increases levels of immune cells that protect the body. Attention, women: Regular sexual activity also jacks up levels of estrogen, a natural antidepressant. Plus, satisfying sex leads to better communication and strengthens relationships, which are two important hedges against depression.

Day 7

Today, plan to get involved in something meaningful. Moods can worsen if you're lonely, isolated, unhappy with your surroundings, or around people who bring you down. You may have to change your lifestyle or make new social contacts. Volunteering is a good way to reduce social isolation and meet new people. Pick a cause you want to support, and volunteer your time and talents to make a difference. You won't be sorry, and you'll feel so much better mentally.

Your mood and thinking can get out of order like any other part of your body. Sometimes, this can make you lose your ability to think normally, feel good, or be happy. The simple daily suggestions I've made here, when built into your lifestyle, will pull you out of a blue funk in no time.

CHAPTER 21
better energy in 7

How many times have you dragged your body out of bed or slogged through the afternoon and thought, "Why? Why do I feel so tired?"

One of the most common complaints women bring to their doctors is: "I feel tired all the time" and "Why do I feel so blah?" Once possible physical causes of fatigue have been ruled out (a crucial first step), many doctors diagnose an energy crisis, pure and simple.

But what is energy exactly? At its most basic level, it's your ability to do work or move, and it comes from the food you eat. But if you've ever come home exhausted after a stressful day only to be instantly revived by your pet's wagging tail or your spouse's open arms, you know feeling energized goes beyond what you had for lunch.

Your energy also ebbs and flows, depending on your stress level, the amount of sleep you get, and how often you exercise. Energy is also affected by your emotional state, as well as your overall sense of well being and satisfaction you feel from the relationships in your life.

The key to maximizing your energy stores is to fill your tank with positive fuel and minimize the things that suck your tank dry. The following are my general recommendations.

Diet

If you want to maintain a good level of energy throughout your day, then the first place you should start is with your diet. The most basic thing to start with is to eliminate foods with refined sugars. There is nothing positive about ingesting refined sugar into your body. It only wears down and weakens your system. You may feel some initial burst of energy, but it won't last, and then you'll feel tired. It's called a sugar high; but, once you come down from the sugar high, you'll become even more tired and less alert. The refined sugar is like an artificial "quick fix" that will end up backfiring on you. So, avoid the refined sugars, and you'll be surprised at how much better you feel and how much more energy you have.

Increase Your Magnesium Intake

Eating a balanced diet can help ensure your vitamin and mineral needs are met. But if you still find yourself too pooped to pop, you could have a slight magnesium deficiency. This mineral is needed for more than 300 biochemical reactions in the body, including breaking down glucose from food into energy. So, when your magnesium levels dip even a little, energy can drop.

The recommended daily intake of magnesium is around 300 milligrams for women and 350 milligrams for men. To make sure you're getting enough, I suggest the following:

- ☐ Take a daily multivitamin/mineral tablet.
- ☐ Add a handful of almonds, hazelnuts, or cashews to your daily diet.
- ☐ Increase your intake of whole grains, particularly bran cereal.
- ☐ Eat more fish; it's loaded with magnesium.

Skip the Nightcap

Alcohol depresses your nervous system—the system of cells, tissues, nerves, and organs that controls your body's responses to the environment around you. So, while sipping a glass of wine or downing a can of beer before bedtime may make you feel like nodding off, the sedative effects wear off as your body metabolizes the alcohol, which may cause you to wake up in the middle of the night and have trouble falling back to sleep. Alcohol has also been shown to interfere with your body's natural 24-hour biorhythms. This causes your blood pressure to jump and heart rate to race at night when it's normally calm and relaxed. You don't have to give up that evening cocktail entirely to achieve sound sleep; just try to avoid alcohol within two to three hours of bedtime.

My Favorite Home Remedies for Energy

Of all the various home remedies for low energy I've come across, one is to take some alfalfa each day. Or, try taking a capsule of bee pollen or ginseng each day for some added energy.

Honey

When you're really dragging and just feel lethargic, one of the simplest ways to combat this problem is to take a daily dose of honey, a natural sugar. You can take honey capsules, or put honey on your toast, or in other foods. Honey is an excellent source of attaining energy. It's natural, and it is has already been digested by bees; thus, it will go right into your blood stream.

Jump

Do you need a jump-start in the morning to get your energy level up? Give yourself a jump-start with a jump. Well, actually, several jumps. Even doing five jumps in the morning will get your blood pumping and your body to wake up. So, start the process of getting your blood flowing and your engine up and roaring by doing jumps!

Take Power Naps

Studies have shown that both information overload and pushing your brain too hard can zap your energy. But studies by the National Institutes of Mental Health found that a 60-minute "power nap" can not only reverse the mind-numbing effects of too much mental exertion, it may also help us to better retain what you have learned and improve your memory in general.

Meditation

Low energy is often brought on by stress. Perhaps one of the most effective ways to eliminate fatigue from our daily lives is to eliminate stress. To do this, think of what causes you the most stress. To overcome stressful situations, try meditation. Meditate for 15 minutes every day. This will help alleviate stress and fatigue in a natural way.

Try Color Therapy

When your eyes see bright hues like red or orange, your pituitary gland pumps up energy production, according to a branch of alternative medicine called color therapy. So, to stay energized, keep these power colors in your line of vision: Buy red tablecloths, keep an orange coffee mug on your desk, or view the world through rose-tinted glasses.

Draining People

I believe that it's important to look at the people in your life. Are they on the go and doing things that charge them? Their enthusiasm can be contagious, lifting your spirit as well. But if they're negative about life or if they're the kind of people who only take from the relationship, they're going to bring you down. You may not be able to stop seeing these folks (they might be relatives!), but by also investing in friendships that broaden your life, you will be able to minimize the effects of the zest killers.

Check Your Thyroid Function and Complete Blood Cell Count

Okay, this is serious doctor advice. If you're constantly low on energy, especially if you feel sluggish even after a good night's rest, talk to your doctor about a blood test for thyroid dysfunction.

Thyroid can be a particular problem for women; it often develops after childbirth and frequently during perimenopause, but a simple blood test can verify whether this is your problem. If you're diagnosed with low thyroid function, medication can bring your body back up to speed.

Now let's look at how to reclaim your energy over the next seven days.

 ## Day 1

You may feel lethargic during the day simply because you don't drink enough water. When you don't drink enough fluid, bacteria and waste products build up in your bladder and show up in your urine. And being even slightly dehydrated can make you feel slow and sluggish. Water helps flush out toxins (like alcohol and tobacco) that can contribute to low energy.

You should aim for eight to ten glasses, so start the day with a glass of warm water and a little lemon juice. Then have a large glass of water every hour for the rest of the day.

The right breakfast will improve concentration and give you a range of essential nutrients. Try scrambled eggs on whole-wheat toast today. Eggs contain all the amino acids essential for energy.

Processed foods like white bread send your energy levels soaring and then rapidly crashing. For lunch, have a sandwich made with whole-grain bread, filled with low-fat protein such as chicken or turkey, followed by plain yogurt and a piece of fruit.

Dragging at 4 p.m.? Sugar and caffeine play havoc with your blood sugar, so avoid coffee and a candy bar. Instead, snack on a handful of nuts and an apple to release energy gradually.

Have a light evening meal tonight and an early night.

📅 Day 2

Start your day with hot water and lemon and then a bowl of oatmeal made with water, topped with flaked almonds, chopped pear, and plain yogurt. The combo of carbs and protein will keep you energized for hours.

Get all mixed up. Drive a different route to work or change your routine in general. Doing things differently can give you extra oomph. Here's why: When you try something new, your brain responds to the exciting stimulus by releasing adrenaline—a natural upper that makes you more alert.

Take a reviving half-hour walk in your lunch hour. Have another protein-rich lunch; try tuna on rye toast with salad and tomatoes.

Find something to laugh about. Research from the University of Maryland School of Medicine found 15 minutes of laughing each day can give your cardiovascular system a workout similar to the effects of exercise, which will boost your energy, as well as cutting your risk of heart disease.

For your evening meal, go for lean protein, such as fish or chicken, with steamed vegetables, avoiding heavy carbs. This will help balance blood sugar so you'll sleep well and wake up full of energy.

📅 Day 3

With your breakfast today, try a vitamin-packed fruit and vegetable juice. Juice three carrots, one apple, half an orange, one stick of celery, and half an inch of fresh ginger.

At lunchtime, try some more vigorous exercise, something that raises your heart rate, such as an aerobics class you can fit into your lunch hour.

If you're stressed over anything, this probably means your emotional energy is running on empty. Squeeze in half an hour for yourself this evening, with a relaxing bath; add some Epsom salts (from pharmacies and health food stores) to help soothe you.

A good night's sleep is crucial to boost energy levels the next day. Avoid TV or computer work before bed; listen to soothing music instead. Research, published in the *Journal of Advanced Learning*, found 45 minutes of soft music lowered heart rate and slowed breathing, all of which will lead to better sleep.

Day 4

For breakfast, try sugar-free muesli with Greek yogurt for a surge of vitality.

Expose yourself to even a few minutes of direct sunlight as soon as you rise. This is a quick way to energize yourself and really wake yourself up. When exposed to natural light, your body recognizes that it's day-time and kicks into high gear. Without a hit of morning sun, you may have that groggy-all-day feeling.

For a variation on the baked spud for lunch, try a baked sweet potato, high in immune-boosting vitamin C. Top with protein such as tuna or cottage cheese, to slow down its energy release.

This evening, give your brain a zap of energy by exercising it with a crossword, sudoku, or even computer games.

Day 5

Have a protein-rich breakfast; then get your day off to an energetic start by walking.

Try some aromatherapy. Sprinkle some drops of zesty lemon essential oil on a tissue and sniff for an instant energy hit. Or, gently press on the palm-side base of your thumb with two fingers for 20 seconds. This reflexology point corresponds with the adrenal reflex, which can cause fatigue when congested.

Try some more exercise this lunch hour, whether it's a swim, a class, or a power-walk. Follow your workout with a nutritious lunch.

Finish your day with a light meal, such as chicken stir-fried with vegetables and nuts, and then have an early night.

This evening, relax in a hot bath with a few drops of ginger essential oil; this will help boost your circulation.

Day 6

For breakfast, try the following blender drink, whiz together 1 banana, 2 apricots, 5 tablespoons of yogurt, 1 tablespoon of whey protein, and 10 teaspoons of apple juice. It's my favorite smoothie for kick-starting the morning.

Take the kids out. Kick a ball around with them, throw a Frisbee, or take them cycling. It'll give you a good combination of exercise, laughter, and fresh air.

For dinner, choose foods rich in magnesium. Try swordfish or cod, both rich in the mineral, with some steamed vegetables.

Saying words that are affirming can help give you a psychological boost. I recommend finding a word that works for you, such as *focus*, *strength*, *power*, or *alert*, and saying it either out loud or to yourself for a quick lift.

Turn on some tunes. Listening to music is one of the most effective ways to increase energy. Research suggests that music effectively distracts you from feeling fatigue. Try burning a CD of your favorite songs and playing it any time you need a pick-me-up. (If you exercise, so much the better, but the music will move you either way.)

Take tummy breaths. When you're under stress, you're prone to take "chest breaths"—short, shallow ones. Chest breathing brings less air into the lungs and reduces the supply of energizing oxygen to the body and brain, leaving you physically and mentally drained. Instead, go for deep, diaphragmatic breathing, like that of a sleeping infant: When you breathe in, your belly should round and fill like a balloon; on an exhale, your belly should slowly deflate.

Day 7

Have a high-protein breakfast like whole-wheat toast and a couple of scrambled eggs.

Declutter. We feel much better when our house is clean and tidy, so use today, or this weekend, to have a good declutter. Go through that teetering pile of papers or overflowing closet and clear stuff out. Clutter can make you feel out of control and overwhelmed, especially when you're already feeling stressed or down.

Go out for a walk. Take in deep lungfuls of air as you walk.

Start winding down early this evening. Sip a cup of chamomile tea before bed, and sprinkle two drops of lavender essential oil on your pillow to help you sleep deeply.

The secrets of physical and mental energy are within your grasp, naturally, effectively, and in just seven days. Give this plan a try, incorporating its suggestions into your lifestyle, and you'll improve your energy level permanently.

7

epilogue

Now you have it: my soup-to-nuts plan to go from "pretty good" to "much better" in just seven days. These are routines and recommendations I've discovered, learned, and gathered over my many years practicing medicine and helping women achieve their beauty goals. These methods work. Whether you're fighting cellulite, a bulging waistline, lack of energy, adult acne, low libido, or any of the other myriad of topics I covered in this book, remember the keyword is better, not perfect! After all, no one is perfect, least of all the models and actresses you see on TV and in the magazines. And unless you have someone walking around behind you fixing your hair, touching up your makeup, adjusting your wardrobe, and airbrushing all your photos, you'll never look like them! Trust me, up-close even they don't look like themselves! But keep up the routines in this book for seven days and beyond, and you'll ultimately discover the "best" version of yourself: someone who feels great, likes what they see in the mirror (even better than if they'd had surgery!), has a true lust for life, and inspires everyone around them to be better themselves. And because you didn't seek the help of a surgeon's scalpel, syringe, or silicone, you'll appreciate your sweet success even more!

about the author

Dr. Andrew Ordon, M.D., F.A.C.S., Plastic & Reconstructive Surgeon and Co-Host of *The Doctors*

Dr. Andrew Ordon is an Emmy®-nominated co-host of the Emmy® award-winning daytime syndicated talk show, *The Doctors*. For over three decades, Dr. Ordon has been an acclaimed surgeon in the areas of aesthetic, plastic, and reconstructive surgery with private practices in New York, Beverly Hills and Rancho Mirage, California. As a co-host of *The Doctors*, Dr. Ordon is best known for delivering the latest medical breakthroughs, cutting-edge practices and newest information on plastic and reconstructive surgery as well as skin care, anti-aging, and health & wellness. Dr. Ordon also shares his work with a number of charities—he is a founding member of the Surgical Friends Foundation—a non-profit surgery organization that provides complimentary reconstructive surgery to patients with serious needs resulting from accidents, burns, and/or congenital defects. He has traveled abroad to perform reconstructive surgeries in Haiti, and cleft palate repairs in India on behalf of Smile Train.

As a medical and plastic surgery expert, Dr. Ordon has appeared on television shows and networks including *Dr Phil*, *The Early Show*, *Rachael Ray*, *20/20*, *Entertainment Tonight*, *48 Hours*, *BBC News*, *CNN*,

NBC News and *ABC News*. He has been quoted in such publications as *Allure, Mademoiselle, Redbook, Glamour* and *Prevention* magazine.

Dr. Ordon is a Phi Beta Kappa graduate of the University of California at Irvine, where he graduated with honors in biological sciences and was the recipient of a National Science Grant for his research in neurophysiology. He then received his medical degree from the USC School of Medicine with honors in medicine. His general surgery training was taken at USC/Los Angeles County Medical Center, followed by a residency program in head and neck surgery at White Memorial/Loma Linda University. Following, Dr. Ordon completed a second residency training program in plastic and reconstructive surgery at the prestigious Lenox Hill Hospital/Manhattan Eye and Ear Infirmary Program in New York City. Affiliated with Cornell University and NYU, this program is recognized as one of the oldest and most renowned centers for aesthetic, plastic and reconstructive surgery in the world.

Dr. Ordon is currently an assistant professor of plastic surgery at Dartmouth School of Medicine and The University of Connecticut. Formerly, he was assistant professor of surgery at both UCLA School of Medicine and The New York Medical College. His hospital affiliations include Cedars-Sinai Medical Center in Los Angeles and Eisenhower Medical Center in Rancho Mirage, Calif. Dr. Ordon is a member of the American Society of Plastic Surgeons, the American Society for Aesthetic Plastic Surgery, the International Society for Aesthetic Plastic Surgery, the Double Boarded Society of Plastic Surgeons and the California Society of Plastic Surgeons. In addition, he is a diplomat of the American Board of Plastic Surgery, the American Board of Otolaryngology & Head and Neck Surgery, the American Board of Cosmetic Surgery and the National Board of Medical Examiners. He is a fellow of the American College of Surgeons, the International College of Surgeons and the American Academy of Facial Plastic and Reconstructive Surgery.

Born in Chicago and raised in Long Beach, CA, Dr. Ordon and his wife divide their time between West Hollywood, New York City and Rancho Mirage. They have two children who are pursuing careers in medicine. In his spare time, Dr. Ordon enjoys surfing, skiing, golf and tennis, boating and travel.

acknowledgements

Thank you to the wonderful producers and staff of *The Doctors* TV show, truly the best in the business. We've been together for four great years, and we really have fun making the show. Much of the inspiration and content for this book were born on that set. And to the creator and executive producer of *The Doctors*, Jay McGraw: Thank you for giving us this platform to not only inform but also entertain our viewers five days a week.